CONSTRUCTING MUSICOLOGY

Constructing Musicology

Alastair Williams

ASHGATE

Published by
Ashgate Publishing Limited
Gower House
Croft Road
Aldershot
Hampshire GU11 3HR
England

Ashgate Publishing Company
Suite 420
101 Cherry Street
Burlington, VT 05401-4405
USA

Ashgate website: http://www.ashgate.com

Reprinted 2003

British Library Cataloguing in Publication Data
Williams, Alastair
Constructing musicology
1. Musicology
I.Title
780.7'2

Library of Congress Control Number: 2001089066

This volume is printed on acid-free paper

ISBN 0 7546 0134 X Pbk

Printed and bound in Great Britain by MPG Books Ltd, Bodmin, Cornwall

Contents

Preface

There is widespread agreement that musicology has recently undergone a paradigm shift; a swing that can be attributed to two not always separable causes: the wider repertoires now studied and the impact of theory on research in the humanities and social sciences. This book attends to both currents, examining and explaining the theoretical issues raised by various musics. Theory is now an area in itself, not necessarily linked to a particular discipline. People who write about Jacques Derrida, for example, may do so in the context of work in literature, art, music, cultural studies or philosophy. Ideas that become theory are ideas that have application beyond the specific domain in which they were formulated, changing the way knowledge is assembled and the sort of claims that people make.[1] For this reason, theory has relevance not only beyond its immediate context of presentation but also beyond academic borders, as it is a mechanism for engaging the codes by which people live and interpret their lives. Within the academy, theory has taken a particularly strong hold in literature departments for the rather theoretical reason that if, as Derrida argues, philosophy or psychoanalysis can be read as text, then interpretation should pay attention to the literary strategies they employ. If message and medium are inextricably linked, then skills of literary interpretation extend far beyond the boundaries of what is normally considered to be literature. It is not, therefore, unreasonable for a literary critic to examine, say, the rhetorical procedures employed by Sigmund Freud.

What would happen if a musicologist were to do this? There is no reason why a theoretically informed musicologist should not chance a reading of, say, Freud's 'Wolf Man' case study, though the result would more likely be understood as a contribution to theory or psychoanalysis than to musicology, unless of course that reading is turned to an issue in music. Musicologists are in a different position from literary critics because they cannot suddenly expand the horizons of their subject to include Freud or Karl Marx, though this constraint should not inhibit (as it once did) Freudian or Marxian readings of music. But in many areas it is not easy to tell where music stops and something else begins, nor is there a compelling reason why someone with a musicological training should not venture into that something else. Should film criticism, for instance, be left entirely to film critics who in some cases pay scant attention to the semiotic function of the score, and should those equipped to comment on the score not be encouraged to expand their views to the film in general? Because a theoretically informed musicology addresses the wide range of discourses and institutions that contribute to musical experience, it is more than likely to wander into other areas. And here it can form fruitful alliances with fields such as art theory that also work at the edges of a dominantly literary culture.

The diversity of areas now feeding musicology ensures that no single person is knowledgeable about them all, and the present author is certainly no exception. Nevertheless, work at a general level can identify themes that touch musicology in ways less evident from more specialized study. For this reason, ethnomusicology debates in the following pages are angled to encompass theoretical issues in general musicology, with more of a focus on method than repertoire. Of these issues, none is more pressing than the boundary itself between musicology and ethnomusicology, which depends on an ever-weakening partition between Western and non-Western cultures. Studying popular music also forces musicology to reassess its disciplinary borders since in this sphere it encounters directly factors such as gender, class and ethnicity that were long neglected. Established criteria such as harmonic originality or structural rigour are frequently not privileged in music that may instead value vocal texture or image; at the same time, the prevalence of recording in this genre challenges critics to re-evaluate ideas of text and performance. Western art music, meanwhile, is represented by a focus on nineteenth- and twentieth-century repertoires; a bias that reflects, arguably, those repertoires in which theoretical developments have been most concentrated, probably because their discourses exert the strongest hold on the ways in which music is understood today.

The much vaunted paradigm shift in musicology can sometimes reach rather self-indulgent proportions that condemn the past without acknowledging earlier work in contextualized musicology. The so-called 'new musicology' can on occasion be at fault on this account, and I have used the term sparingly (preferring the more neutral 'current musicology') because some 'new' themes are really rather old, and because even the new ages. In Britain the term 'critical musicology' has been coined to describe recent developments in musicology, particularly within the field of popular music studies, and it usefully designates a critical orientation. The nomenclature is used here to convey a musicology willing to reflect on its institutions and practices, but more often I have simply referred to theory, sharing a widespread humanities parlance. I do so in the knowledge that some musicologists are undoubtedly more theoretically inclined than others, but do not consider theory to be of relevance only to a specialist minority. On the contrary, its reach traverses the whole field since music is a human construct that demands interpretation. (It should be mentioned at this stage, since musicology includes an area dubbed theory and analysis, that I am talking about what is widely understood as theory in the humanities and regard 'music theory' as a section within this much wider field.)

Theory has exerted a now irrevocable impact on musicology, hence musicologists face the challenge of understanding a wide range of theory and applying it to their own interests. With this task in mind, this book aims both to gain a place for musicology in theory debates and to negotiate a theoretical position for musicology. This is a double process: in one mode it opens channels so that musicology may feed aspects of theory that are of general interest, in the other it bring the rigours of theory to bear on the aims and methodologies of musicology. The result is not a prototype musicology, but a musicology that reflects on its own procedures and creates strategies for particular problems; in short a musicology under construction.

The sometimes caricatured exchanges between old and new musicologies echo binary distinctions between modernism and postmodernism, meta and micro narratives, closed and decentred subjects.[2] Modernism and postmodernism are discussed in more detail in Chapter 6, but some initial exposition is necessary at this stage. Strictly speaking, they are the cultural manifestations of the wider project of modernity and postmodernity. The beginning of modernity is hard to date precisely, and can be traced back to the Reformation. The Enlightenment, however, marks an important stage by attempting systematically to apply rational criteria to all domains of knowledge.

Deploying a philosophy of consciousness, it contends that human beings are subjects who interact with the world of objects, comprehending them according to shared perceptual apparatus, and thereby regulating both themselves and the world around them.[3] In this scheme of things, morality and art are deemed to embody essential human values and characteristics. Postmodernity questions the confidence of such assumptions, asking whether the subject can really understand the world and itself so transparently, and enquiring whether universal values represent the values of the powerful imposed on the less powerful. Strongly influenced by Michel Foucault, postmodernity often depicts the institutions of modernity as forms of internal repression rather than liberation, so that the utopian dream of Enlightenment becomes more like a nightmare. And such a view can find plenty to sustain it in the policing of subjectivity. Problems arise when this sort of critique rejects modernity *tout court* as totalitarian and can therefore advance no grounds for rational agreement, offering in its place an unsustainable relativism and decentred subjectivity. My argument is that if such binary extremes are deconstructed, then the critical legacy of modernity can be reconstructed, and offer much of value to musicology today.

Chapter 1 opens with a discussion of traditional musicology in the context of Joseph Kerman's call for a shift from fact finding to critical interpretation. It then turns to Theodor Adorno's and Carl Dahlhaus's scrutiny of the bourgeois tradition, touching, in Adorno's case, on debates about modernity that resonate with later chapters. Kerman's critique of structural analysis is taken further in Chapter 2, where formalist analysis is examined as proto-structuralist methodology, thereby linking its claims to a wide range of disciplines. Subsequently, I assess the impact of poststructuralism on musicology before turning to more general issues in the semiotics of music. Chapter 3 examines how gender is constructed in music, and considers the once neglected history of music by women. It closes by assessing the relevance of psychoanalytical theory to musical understanding.

Moving into the field of popular music, Chapter 4 opens with classic critiques of the culture industry and turns to the idea of popular music as a form of resistance to imposed ideology. After discussing notions of authenticity, it picks up themes from Chapter 3 in particular, concluding with a section on how identity and image are negotiated in song. Continuing the operatic focus of Chapter 3, Chapter 5 contemplates the way non-European cultures are represented by

European culture and leads to an examination of debates within ethnomusicology. What, it asks, does it mean for Westerners to study the music of non-Westerners, and does this process automatically impose a form of knowledge that distorts as it informs? These questions echo the preoccupation in gender studies with how identity generates notions of inside and outside, self and other. Chapter 6 turns to modernity, a theme that has underpinned much of the previous discussion (and its opening section might usefully be read after the Preface by anyone seeking information on the larger debates in which musicology is situated). Examining the emergence of the modern subject and its formation in music, it argues that postmodernism is better understood as a transformation of modernism than as its antithesis. This argument parallels my view that current musicology should tap continuities with earlier critical approaches, and should be willing to scrutinize its own claims more closely. No area is more contested than canonic prestige, so I close by proposing a form of reception that might emancipate Beethoven's Fifth Symphony from the pompous, grandiose claims made in its name. I do so with a view to asserting the value of music as a medium through which we can negotiate identities and meanings.

My overall aim is to show the forces at work in current musicology, to demonstrate that traditions are socially constructed, and to suggest that established beliefs can be transformed in a theoretically flexible environment.

I am grateful to *Music Analysis* for allowing me to draw on material that originally appeared in this journal, and which benefited from the editing skills of Alan Street ('Musicology and Postmodernism', 19/3, 2000). I should like to thank Daniel Chua, Michael Spitzer, Katharine Ellis, Dai Griffiths, Jonathan Stock and Ian Biddle, each of whom read a chapter in manuscript. I was much heartened by their readiness to set aside time from busy schedules to provide comments on various topics, and am much indebted for the advice they offered. I am also grateful to Giles Hooper for reading a whole draft and making useful suggestions, and am obliged to Ian Phillips-Kerr for setting the music examples. Thanks, also, to Jim Samson and Anthony Pople for supporting this project. A much appreciated research award from Keele University provided the time for writing. Wendy and Oliver, meanwhile, provided a sustaining home environment.

1 Traditions

One of the main ideas in this book is that music is embedded in discourses and surrounded by ideas that contribute to its meaning. Musicology, therefore, is as old as music: you cannot have one without the other because musicology is simply a category for some of the discourses and views held about music. Having said this, however, it is true that certain forms of knowledge have to be in place before musicology emerges as a distinct domain. Musicology as a recognized academic discipline is quite young, and a celebrated exposition of its purpose is found in Guido Adler's 'Umfang, Methode und Ziel der Musikwissenschaft' of 1885 (Musicology's Scope, Method and Aim).

A product of the nineteenth-century German enthusiasm for encyclopaedic knowledge, Adler's new discipline of *Musikwissenschaft* (science of music) draws on positivist influences from the social sciences and literary philology, with a view to categorizing and summarizing all existing knowledge about music.[1] In doing so, it divides the study of music into two main areas: historical musicology and systematic musicology, the former concerned with Western art music, the latter turning to acoustics, psychology, sociology, aesthetics and comparative musicology (the term used for what later became ethnomusicology). Adler acknowledges that all cultures with music also have theories about music, but this awareness does not stop him from expecting his own systematic categories to have applications to all types of music, not just to the European tradition. Here begin some of the problems that have vexed later musicology, since even though Adler fails to theorize the historical location of his own ideas, he nevertheless considers the scholarly tools derived from a European, specifically German, culture applicable to all traditions. The result, despite broad-minded intentions, was that history-based study of European music, with the

Austro-German tradition at its heart, came to constitute the centre of musicology.

That canon is a central concern for all three of the figures discussed in this chapter (namely Kerman, Adorno and Dahlhaus), but they also share a willingness to examine the methodologies used to study this music and to question the claims made on its behalf. It is this reflexivity that makes them significant figures and which (directly in Kerman's case) leads into debates in current musicology.

Kerman

Historical study of European art music was formative in the development of musicology in North America (which was heavily influenced by German émigrés), notwithstanding the efforts of Charles Seeger to establish an American musicology that exemplified the inclusive aspect of Adler's systematic musicology while breaking away from European repertoire.[2] The subsequent struggle to create a more inclusive practice of musicology partly derives from a desire to recognize American traditions, including folk, popular, art and indigenous musics. It is also a reflection of a post-cold war Europe trying to re-evaluate its cultural inheritance. Nevertheless, when Joseph Kerman (1924–) wrote his landmark study of post-war musicology in America and Britain (published as *Musicology* in Britain and *Contemplating Music* in the USA), he was still able to make distinctions between the historical study of Western art music, theory and analysis, and ethnomusicology, reserving the term musicology for the first one only, thereby placing its concerns dead centre. In so doing, he reflected a divide between a mainstream historical musicology and what was traditionally called systematic musicology. (Formalist analysis would definitely fit into the systematic category, though Adler himself saw it as an adjunct to the history of style.)

This slicing of music's research areas articulates distinctions in repertoire, and in historical, structural and anthropological methodologies, but little is gained by reserving the term 'musicology' for one repertoire and methodology only. This is because historical musicology, analysis and ethnomusicology can all be placed under the rubric of musicology; indeed Kerman acknowledges this on one level by arguing that they all suffer from the baleful influences of modernism. Furthermore, a clear division between musicology and ethnomusicology now looks increasingly shaky, since it rests on premisses of musical ownership and suggests that the study of

Western music need not be concerned with ethnicity. Far better, then, to think of musicology as a general field that turns its attention to particular repertoires, using a variety of methodologies.

Kerman's book is often considered to be a watershed, marking the divide between old and new musicologies in a schema that usefully reflects a change in orientation, but can lead to exaggerated claims. The 'before and after' pattern is encouraged by his tendency to attribute musicology's most rigid paradigms to modernist ideology. Despite differing preoccupations, he argues, both analysis and positivist musicology share an interest in employing quasi-scientific methodologies to jettison Romantic aesthetics and to slough off woolly associations between musical meaning and the composer's biography. Specious though the claims to scientific objectivity made on behalf of the old-style positivist musicology may be, Kerman acknowledges that reliable editions of music are a necessary preliminary to the critical commentary he hopes will ensue. Since musicology lagged behind the editorial projects of literary philology, much work was needed and musicologists were trained diligently to carry out these tasks.

The rationale for this activity, argues Kerman, was provided by Arthur Mendel, a Bach scholar and Professor of Music at Princeton University, in a paper entitled 'Evidence and Explanation', delivered in 1961 at the New York Congress of the International Musicology Society. Following models developed in analytical philosophy, Mendel sought to establish laws for the causal deduction of musical facts, asking how one can be derived from another. His paper suggested that one could generate a continuum between the establishment of a fact such as the date of an autograph, and more general ideas such as the influence of one composer on another. In practice, however, scholars were reluctant to progress beyond factual detail to interpretive schemes. Lamenting this state of affairs and suggesting that musicology should move a step up the interpretive ladder, Kerman opens a distinction between scholarship and criticism, arguing that the former should become more like the latter. His hope is that musicologists will become more engaged with music as experience rather than as object, with a view to assessing (like literary critics) the value of music and demonstrating its cultural importance.

Kerman's model for criticism is literary in origin, but it turns to theory and analysis for specific guidance. Less interested in theoretical models of tonality, for example, than in analysis of particular pieces, Kerman (writing in the early 1980s) regards analysis as the area most likely to achieve the prestige that criticism enjoys in literature, even though his enthusiasm is driven more by its potential than actuality. Princeton also proved to be a dominant force in this field, with Mendel's colleague the composer and theorist Milton Babbitt exerting huge institutional influence. His work binds composition and theory together in a search for the development and understanding of new musical techniques. Under the auspices of a quasi-scientific model of composition, the theory and production of new music became established in universities as research activities to be communicated to a specialist, informed audience. (Earlier, positivist musicology had likewise found a place in the academy by aligning itself with the established historical and philological concerns of other humanities disciplines.) Babbitt's ideas were eventually given a specifically theoretical turn away from direct compositional application by Allen Forte's set theory (explained in the next chapter), which sought to apply high modernist discoveries about the ordering of pitch-class sets to the analysis of earlier twentieth-century music, particularly that by Schoenberg.

The other main field in theory and analysis, in which Forte was again a leading player, was the formulation and institutionalization of ideas devised by Heinrich Schenker (also discussed in the next chapter) for the analysis of tonal music. Schenkerian methodology, with its structural preoccupations, is intimately linked to the values built into the reception history of the Austro-German canon. In a circular process, it prizes music characterized by structural coherence, and by honing analytical tools to find these features reaffirms the prestige of the same music, placing Bach and Beethoven at the centre of its orbit. Geared to a particular repertoire, the values built into the technique not only enhance this canon, but serve to exclude musics that fail to meet these criteria, typically musics more firmly rooted in performance than in text. This key distinction is put, in slightly different terms, by Dahlhaus (of whom more later), who talks of the twin styles in nineteenth-century music, referring to the German, instrumental style of Beethoven and the Italian opera style of Rossini.[3] If Beethoven claimed for his music the strong concept of art rooted in text, argues Dahlhaus, Rossini's style uses the score as a recipe for performance, understanding music as an event rather than text. A canon based on authorial intention and textual accuracy will, then, automatically value Beethoven's model above Rossini's. In this respect, analytical methodology shares with positivist musicology a tendency to fetishize the text, as if it were the only dimension in which music exists.

This shared tendency led Kerman to conflate positivism and formalism in a confusing manner.[4] Both contribute to canonic prestige and both seek scientific rigour, but there are important differences. Preparing manuscripts and studying sources are, or were, exercises dependent on the idea of authorial intention, with editions allegedly representing the design of the composer and eliminating the contingencies that occur in performance. Such activities do not presume a direct link between autobiography and music, but they may well pay attention to details of the composer's life as a way of accumulating more factual information about a particular score, such as when it was completed or first performed. Schenkerian analysis and set theory, by contrast, seek internal structure rather than authorial intention (as we shall see in the next chapter) and are not especially concerned about historical detail. For although Schenker was clearly influenced by extraneous factors and was a champion of the *Urtext*, his primary interest was the way deep-rooted properties of tonality (expressed in the *Ursatz*) present themselves in a score. Set theory, meanwhile, seeks underlying governors that facilitate particular permutations from the whole range of possible pitch-class combinations. Removed from time, both approaches pursue fundamental principles, a preoccupation that passed from nineteenth-century notions of autonomy and unity to modernist aesthetics. The underlying coherence that formalism values is, therefore, not directly comparable to the historical data sought by positivism. Analysis, according to Kerman, is potentially nearer the criticism he envisages because it involves active engagement with the music and demands decisions on matters of primary and secondary importance. Even though editing might entail interpretation and judgement, standard practice tried to minimize their range rather than explore their creative potential.[5]

Kerman's critique of the text-based obsessions of positivist musicology and formalist analysis is now a common theme in musicology. It has received particular attention from Richard Taruskin, who detects in the efforts to objectify texts a downgrading of the human subjectivity (including performing traditions) in which music is always suspended. The search for a pure text, he suggests, is like cleaning a revered painting, stripping away the dust and accumulated restorations. By removing the 'dirt' from music, he maintains, musicologists destroy what other human beings have made of the music.[6] A comparable desire to understand texts as events in which human participation is transparent can be found in the frustrations of ethnomusicologists with positivist musicology. For a musicology less fascinated by the prospect of science-like objectivity, however, the gap between music as event and as object need not be severe. Notation, like sounding music, is a configuration of subjectivity. When this dimension is understood to contribute to, rather than control, musical experience, it need not inhibit more obviously participatory forms of subjectivity.

Kerman hopes that historical musicology and analysis can leave behind their objectivizing tendencies and form an amalgam that will lead to what he calls a 'musicology oriented towards criticism'.[7] This model, though he does not say so, is very close to the vision that tantalizes Dahlhaus, namely a history of music that is both capable of standing up to historiographical scrutiny and has something to say about the actuality of music. As we shall see, Dahlhaus's pursuit of this goal led him into considerations of historiography, sociology and hermeneutics that are largely untouched by Kerman.[8] The model Kerman envisages derives from literary criticism, a field fully aware of the theoretical concerns, amongst others, that Dahlhaus addresses. *Musicology* mentions developments in semiotics, deconstruction and feminism in literary studies and expects them to impact on musicology,[9] but does not take its lead from then recently published books such as Edward Said's *Orientalism* or Jonathan Culler's *On Deconstruction*. Despite noting Culler's call for an end of interpretation in literary studies,[10] Kerman goes on to say that there is plenty of scope for interpretation in the less extensively mined field of musicology; by doing so he underestimates the impact a theoretically empowered reader exerts on traditional interpretation, even in an uncrowded discipline. The type of criticism Kerman recommends is more like what used to be mainstream literary criticism – a patchwork of analysis, criticism, history and, possibly, aesthetics that would link music to underlying human values.

Writing at the beginning of the 1990s, and contemplating developments since the publication of *Musicology*, he shifts his emphasis. Kerman now acknowledges that the paragraph in the Introduction about musicology travelling some distance behind modern theory would have to be rewritten in the light of contemporary developments.[11] He then argues that such transformations should not be understood as a splintering of musicology since they are increasingly becoming the central concerns of the discipline. By making this point, he acknowledges that what he had envisaged as a turn to criticism heralded a full-scale application of postmodernist theory to musicology; a process that is changing the discipline permanently and enabling it to participate in important debates beyond the conventional borders of musicology. With expanding, multiple canons and changing methodologies, the fluid boundaries of musicology merge into other disciplines, enabling more interdisciplinary work. This state of affairs does not make traditional fact-finding missions obsolete, since newly opened repertoires create plenty of work of this type. It does, however, demand that such projects push beyond the mechanical application of a methodology towards interpretive conclusions. Musicology has taken the turn that Kerman called for, therefore, though in not quite the manner he envisaged. His study remains a valuable document for its inside knowledge of people involved in the field and for its demand that musicology understand its own institutions.

Most of the present book, particularly the later chapters, is concerned with the directions musicology has taken after the publication of Kerman's appraisal; nevertheless it is important to understand that many of the so-called new themes were in currency well before the 1980s. Adorno and Dahlhaus are mentioned by Kerman, but due to his explicit Anglo-American axis they receive only limited attention. Both figures deal with major themes such as canon and autonomy in sophisticated ways that, in varying degrees, still have relevance today. Turning to Adorno first, we find a leading theorist of modernity investigating musical subjectivity in the context of significant intellectual debates.

Adorno

Theodor Adorno (1903–69) was a member of the Frankfurt Institute of Social Research (better known as the Frankfurt School of Critical Theory), which sought to extend Marxian ideology critique beyond the confines of economics to areas such as psychoanalysis and, especially in Adorno's case, cultural analysis. Adorno's ideas have relevance on two fronts for musicology: on one he is a major twentieth-century cultural critic; so as musicology becomes part of wider cultural debates, his views on culture in conditions of modernity become part of the reservoir from which musicology can draw.[12] Adorno is also of relevance to musicology in the second, more obvious, sense that over half his huge output is devoted to music criticism. Music was of huge importance to him and many of his ideas on aesthetics were formulated in this medium. The two sides of Adorno create a dilemma for musicologists: those wishing to access his opinions of, say, Berg (with whom he took composition lessons) are drawn into a philosophical labyrinth, while those primarily interested in his methodology become entangled in musical polemics. The two strands are not easily separated since his ideas characteristically tend to pull in several directions. Knowledge of both sides is necessary for full appreciation of Adorno's ideas, since one cannot understand what he has to say about music without being towed into major debates about modernity.

It might be gleaned from the above discussion that Adorno occupies an ambiguous position in relation to the methodologies discussed in this book, since (despite continuing interest in his work) awareness of how his ideas relate to current musicology is patchy. Acceptance in Anglo-American musicology of the critical methodology that informs Adorno's music writings has been slow for a number of reasons: its resistance to positivist and formalist approaches; the difficulty of his style; and the limited availability (until recently) of translations. Adorno is now read more widely, but his writings still resist assimilation, whether by traditional or newer musicologies. Too subjective for formalist analysis and too modernist for the 'new musicology', Adorno is vulnerable to critique from many positions. With his adherence to the Austro-German tradition, he can be accused of defending an elitist canon that excludes other musics and identities, of showing intolerance towards popular music, and of possessing little inclination to consider non-European musics. In short, he laments the decline of European culture as if it were the only culture worth discussing.

Espousing so many of the values that the new musicology has challenged, he might seem a paradigm of the bad old ways – a tortured Tovey with little to offer current musicology. But at the same time – and Adorno is all about simultaneous contradictions – he pioneered the application of critical theory to musicology and his understanding of music as encrypted subjectivity anticipates current thinking. The problem is that his most old-fashioned beliefs and most prescient insights often stand side by side. It is hard to digest what is useful and move on because, as a theorist with interests that extend well beyond musicology, he remains awkwardly ahead of the field, providing a critical legacy from which to understand the postmodernist dysfunctions that extend to musicology. More precisely, he uncovers the contradictions of bourgeois aesthetics, but uses its rational core to expose the paradoxes of using market forces as a measure of cultural value.

Before addressing Adorno's aesthetics of music in particular, it would be useful to consider what the Frankfurt School means by the term 'ideology critique'. 'Ideology' is a confusing term used in a variety of ways, and in some current parlance it simply functions as a synonym for opinion – for whatever one happens to believe. Such casual usage is hugely at variance with the classical Marxist concept of false consciousness: the idea (which has some similarities to Freudian notions of the unconscious) that people absorb the conditions of material and social production in a way that obscures how the latter serve the interests of a minority at the expense of the majority. Thus, the argument goes, it is only when people are able to understand the forces that shape their lives on a conscious level that they will possess the means, and will, to change them. This argument is often criticized for making blanket assumptions about ideological delusion, even so we can retain from it the core idea that ideology contains a degree of mystification, and resist simplistic reductions of the term to mean personal opinion.

The Marxist model of ideology critique is most evident in Adorno's work on popular music, functioning to unmask social constructions that are presented as natural, disinterested beliefs or procedures. Understood thus, ideology critique remains a vital concept for current theory, clearly seen in, say, feminism's analysis of the way patriarchal attitudes are built into accepted social institutions. Consequently, it is also of relevance to recent approaches in musicology, since so many of them endeavour to show the assumptions at work in traditional musicological beliefs. Ideology critique aims to socialize ingrained attitudes not because it believes that human beings have no essential attributes, but because it is convinced that most of these are encountered in historically specific ways. Socialization does not immediately dissolve entrenched standpoints, but it does render them susceptible to contestation and transformation. When, for example, we examine the ways musicological beliefs are assembled, they do not automatically collapse – they become porous to different outlooks.

Ideology critique in Adorno's music aesthetics draws on an intricate network of (mainly German) sociological, philosophical and critical traditions, which are often unacknowledged and seldom explained. At the end of his life, however, Adorno did formulate many of the ideas to be found in his music criticism in *Aesthetic Theory*, a posthumously published manuscript that he was still editing at the time of his death. One cannot pretend that this sophisticated theory of modernist art is easy to understand, nevertheless with perseverance it does provide a clarifying framework for the music writings. The title itself is significant because 'aesthetics', with its elitist connotations, is not a widely used term nowadays in the fields of critical and cultural theory, since it evokes a rarified branch of philosophy concerned with the appreciation of art and nature. Kant's *Critique of Judgement*, a core text in the study of aesthetics, is concerned with the disinterested contemplation of beauty and taste, with little to say on the production or meaning of art. In Adorno's hands, these categories are modified so that they become social constructions rather than universal categories. From the perspective of Frankfurt critical theory, categories of beauty and taste contribute to the discourses of art rather than remaining neutral concepts.

Like aesthetics, music, for Adorno, is a social medium through and through. The explanation he fomulates for this thesis is that musical material is a sedimentation, or mediation, of subjectivities and social practices. Musical material congeals and shapes an ensemble of social practices in a medium with its own characteristics. Consequently, when we encounter music we encounter socialized energies.[13] These forces are frequently obvious in popular music, but remain more encrypted in Western art-music traditions. In the latter case, social absorption can lead to abstract results (a Schoenberg string quartet, say), encouraging us to talk about material in a self-referential manner, however socialized it might be. Nevertheless, all music is socially situated in more direct ways, since it is maintained by institutions such as concert halls, orchestras, arts management and audiences, and meanings arise from intersections of these various currents. In popular music, it may well be the social context of its performance and reception that is of prime importance. The message or mode of subjectivity, that is to say, may be carried less in the notes and more in the environment associated with various genres.[14]

This conclusion is indebted to Adorno even though it is somewhat at variance with his own negative view of popular music as a form of industrialized deception. In his popular music criticism at least, he remained too dependent on the idea of a socialized material and paid little attention to the more obviously social elements of its environment. Popular music, for him, is an administered culture governed by a system that cannot fulfil the desire it generates. Because his aesthetics (especially of new music) is so reliant on advanced material – a material that offers a critical perspective on socio-historical conditions – he is often blind to the possibility of popular practices being at any variance with standardized modes of production. This limitation is a reflection of his theory of social mediation, which assumes that a single set of social configurations will find their way into material, and is on a larger scale symptomatic of an undifferentiated application of ideology critique. Because contemporary societies are too stratified for their forms to be embodied in a particular type of material, the idea of mediation needs to be adjusted to accommodate multiple social groups with different aesthetic aspirations. This said, however, the larger steering mechanisms of modernity traverse many social groups and can perhaps be projected into problems of musical form.

Even though Adorno places a high premium on artistic autonomy, he does so in a dialectical construction that is far removed from social transcendence. He both defends and breaches autonomy because he believes that musical material possesses its own dynamics, makes its own demands, and can be understood in its own terms; but simultaneously argues that the ideal of self-containment and self-determinacy is an illusory projection of the bourgeois subject. Holding in tension two opposing views that are nevertheless dependent on each other is typical of Adorno's dialectical method, which differs from classical Hegelian dialectics in not seeking a synthesizing progression. By allowing incompatible views of musical material to tug at each other, Adorno is able to argue that when experience is distilled through material it can generate a dynamic of its own that enjoys some critical distance from the prevailing instrumental rationality.

As a theorist of modernity, one of Adorno's main themes is that all aspects of our lives are increasingly dominated by a form of reason – instrumental reason – bent on administering and measuring the world to such an extent that the process becomes self-perpetuating. The consequence is that subjects become alienated from both the world and from each other, losing sight of the human goals that such practices are supposed to serve.[15] In the light of such tendencies, he values music's claim to autonomy because the lack of social purpose it gains is not immediately compatible with instrumental aims. And this distance, however illusory it may be, enables music to pursue social codes in directions blocked by the prevailing imperative. Adorno's sensitivity to what is suppressed and dominated in the name of reason does not, however, lead him to advocate music as a realm of irrational release, since it offers instead a domain in which sensuous detail can share the same space as formal coherence.

This dialectical reading of bourgeois music resists a brand of cultural studies that can only find in the canon an array of distasteful ideologies. The latter view labours under the misapprehension that music, because it is a carrier of social forms, is somehow tainted, and provides a mirror image of the equally untenable belief that music is a realm of pure sonic relationship unburdened by referentiality. Adorno's point is that while music cannot float free of ideological baggage, it can expose such attitudes to experiences that would normally be expelled by their patterns of exclusion, since formal coherence is not equivalent to the hegemonic imposition of a single idea. This view finds more concrete realization in recent forms of musicology. Lawrence Kramer, for example, has examined the constructions of subjectivity that inhabit Schubert's songs, placing particular emphasis on the articulation of gender.[16]

Having established the framework in which Adorno's music criticism takes place, while noting that particular aspects become malleable when confronted with his own preferences, we can now turn to his writings on music. The main monographs are on Beethoven (a posthumous collection of essays and fragments), Wagner, Mahler, Berg, Stravinsky and Schoenberg (the last two, combined, make up *Philosophy of Modern Music*). In each of these studies Adorno attempts to crack the social codes of the music: to show how the subject is represented in conditions of modernity. In middle-period Beethoven he finds an embodiment of the self-determining subject and a distillation of a society in which the reconciliation of the part and the whole, of individual aspirations and social organization, briefly seemed an attainable goal. Adorno particularly values the compatibility of motivic identity and larger formal functions in this music – the balance, that is to say, between the particular and the whole. In the late style, Adorno argues – and with particular relevance for subsequent modernist developments – the ultimately illusory nature of such a dialectical synthesis becomes apparent, and consequently the musical language becomes less compatible with established forms. A more interiorized music, which glows from within, indicates a subjectivity withdrawn from the instrumental world.

In the case of Wagner, Adorno detects a contradictory situation whereby the bourgeois subject is inflated to mythological proportions by an art-form that bears witness to the industrial processes of its day. Wagner anticipates not only the technical possibilities pursued by modernism but also, through an all-engulfing art-form, the mass culture that accompanied them. In contrast to the polemics born of admiration that mark the Wagner monograph, Adorno's study of Mahler, written late in his life, is a sensitive portrait of a composer with whom he clearly felt deep empathy. This admiration stems from the capacity of Mahler's symphonies to reflect on their own procedures.[17] It enabled Adorno to modify some of the principles that he rigorously applies elsewhere, notably the insistence on advanced material, which is here softened by arguing that Mahler releases new latency from apparently obsolete devices. Adorno's Mahler stands on the cusp of modernism, but retains nostalgia for the illusion of symphonic synthesis. Likewise, this figure's relations with the autonomy principle are also awkward: he makes symphonic form an environment of its own, while including elements such as folk and café musics that would normally lie outside the domain of this genre, rubbing against the symphonic logic.

Written in exile from Nazi Germany, *Philosophy of Modern Music* remains Adorno's most famous polemic. In stark terms it portrays Schoenberg as the embodiment of an alienated, modern subject, with Stravinsky as its depleted, mechanized antipode. When this book is read as a dialectic of modernity, with Schoenberg and Stravinsky representing irreconcilable strands,[18] it remains of great interest (despite Adorno's obvious prejudices) because it addresses the fate of the bourgeois subject and its cultural forms in an increasingly mechanized age. Schoenberg's response to this predicament, according to Adorno, is that the subject, so as to avoid complete subjugation, becomes immersed in material procedures, finding a certain freedom in the objectified forms of technical procedure. Stravinsky's answer, by contrast, is to separate material from tradition, organizing it externally in a search for novel, unexpected configurations. Adorno detects a potential critical trace in this approach, especially in the surrealist proclivities of *The Soldier's Tale*, but his overwhelming opinion is that such detachment, particularly in the neo-classical works, is symptomatic of a drained modern subjectivity. Even in the Russian works, notably in the unforgiving narrative of *Petrushka*, he finds the faceless steering forces of modernity, with no human impulse to offset them. Whatever we make of this reading – and the cruelty of the puppet play cannot be dismissed – its message is that the codes of modernity have an insidious habit of always being present in one guise or another.

This capacity to understand music as encrypted subjectivity, even as a carrier of ideology, makes Adorno's significance for musicology immense. While we may disagree with some of his judgements and regret his tunnel vision, much that is deemed new in current musicology is to be found in Adorno's music criticism. It is true that the specific routes through which subjectivity is now explored, such as gender and ethnicity, are not central themes in his work, but they are commensurate with his insistence that generalized procedures should heed the needs of the particular. It is also true that Adorno remains faithful to a philosophy of consciousness, with its language of Subject and Object, whereas contemporary theory follows the linguistic turn, understanding discourses in semiotic terms (as explained in the next chapter). But the positions can communicate because what Adorno calls a concept, the synthesis of Subject and Object, is comparable to what semiotics calls a sign-unit, the synthesis of signifier and signified.[19] Moreover, it is possible in both traditions to resist mechanisms that impose uniformity. Nevertheless, the politics of identity have changed since Adorno's era. By exploring the particular in more concrete ways and by rejecting the limitations of the age in which Adorno lived, musicology has overtaken some of his preoccupations. His fear of an administered society retains substance, but his analysis of its manifestations underestimates the complex differentiation of society and its capacity to produce unpredictable cultural forms. In another sense, however, he remains as important as ever, particularly in the age of globalization, for his determination to think though the social totality, for his insistence that abstract procedures should not eliminate individual needs, and for his willingness to value affinities as well as differences.[20]

Dahlhaus

Carl Dahlhaus (1928–89) and Adorno were acquaintances and shared a penchant for wide reading. While trying to steer musicology away from overtly sociological concerns, Dahlhaus nevertheless built on

Adorno's achievements. Before returning to Dahlhaus's engagement with Adorno, it is worth sketching the components of what James Hepokoski has called 'The Dahlhaus Project'.[21] This undertaking is rooted in the intellectual climate of German cultural debates in the 1960s and 1970s, and shares the now prevalent willingness – if not the values – of a musicology keen to participate in mainstream humanities concerns. The focus of Dahlhaus's prolific output is the European canon, and its associated discourses. Such themes form the basis of *Foundations of Music History*, which is generally taken to be the key text regarding his methodological concerns and provides a standard against which more practical projects such as *Nineteenth-Century Music* can be assessed.

By interrogating historical methodology, Dahlhaus challenges traditional attempts to make musical meaning a function of its composer's biography and develops a healthy wariness of so-called objective historical data. The so-called neutral fact is in his view already situated in a network of assumptions, and only really derives meaning from the narrative context in which it is embedded. Consequently, were the sentence 'On 19 October 1814 Franz Schubert composed his "Gretchen am Spinnrade" ('Gretchen at the Spinning-Wheel') to occur at the beginning of a chapter in a music history, he argues, it would convey more information than this fact, since 'it expresses a view as to the origins of the romantic lied'.[22] The construction of history is therefore a selective process whereby certain facts are given more priority than others, producing a narrative flow in the process. Because the linking of occurrences in the mind of the historian will never mirror what he calls an 'actual sequence of causes', the same facts can be accommodated by conflicting value judgements.[23] Therefore, Dahlhaus argues, the historian has no option but to engage methodological problems, since they will always plague positivist research. However, he is aware that such complexities can paralyse scholarship and offsets methodological reflexivity with a pragmatism willing to adapt strategies to particular situations. For this reason, what may sometimes look like a lack of consistency or conviction is upheld by his belief that a single method is not appropriate for all historical problems.

His theoretical approach to music history is matched by an interest in music aesthetics. Classical aesthetics has been attacked by recent musicologies, but Dahlhaus's work in this area informed his view, now widely shared, that perceptions of music are heavily influenced by (sometimes invisible) discourses. Adopting a position closer to ideology critique than he might have acknowledged, Dahlhaus argues that those who dismiss aesthetics as idle speculation divorced from the realities of music frequently, unknown to themselves, espouse views shaped by an aesthetic discourse with a specific historical derivation. He was able to open *The Idea of Absolute Music*, written in the mid-1970s, in this vein by showing how 'common sense', accepted views on music derive from what he calls a music-aesthetic paradigm of absolute music. Those reluctant to read the programme associated with a tone poem or the plot of an opera, he maintains, are governed by an aesthetic belief that music transcends verbal interpretation; a judgement directly indebted to the aesthetics of absolute music (and hotly contested by current musicology).[24] Dahlhaus does not overturn this inherited opinion, but he certainly destabilizes it since there is an inherent contradiction in the idea that absolute music, which is supposed to inhabit a realm untroubled by the material world, should be dependent on a historically located aesthetic. By studying music from the perspective offered by its time and by addressing subsequent developments, he both inhabits and critiques the aesthetic of absolute music.

This in-between status is also characteristic of Dahlhaus's work on two ideas closely related to the aesthetics of absolute music: autonomy and the canon. Linking autonomy to the institution of the bourgeois concert, which crystallized in the eighteenth century,[25] he is fully aware of the mechanisms by which such conventions arose, but also committed to justifying their claims. His compromise is what he calls 'relative autonomy' – the belief that music possesses its own procedures but is also open to various historical processes.[26] He is also keenly aware of the procedures by which canons are assembled, noting that it was the nineteenth-century fascination with autonomy that secured a prime place for Bach.[27] But this circumstance, though it came about through historical interpretation, is not something that can be reversed, according to Dahlhaus, since the canon reaches us with the authority of tradition, and is therefore something we receive rather than make.

In order to take Dahlhaus's view on the canon (and much else) further it is necessary at this point to examine the intricate connections between his ideas and theories advanced by Hans-Georg Gadamer and his student Hans Robert Jauss. Grappling with similar problems, these two theorists sought a path between the twin poles of positivism and sociology by working in the tradition of hermeneutics (the study of interpretation). Gadamer is discussed in *Foundations of Music History*, but neither the summary nor the following critique indicates how firmly the central planks of his *magnum opus*, *Truth and Method*, are lodged in Dahlhaus's writings. Like Dahlhaus, Gadamer discredits the objective claims of positivist historicism, bringing two factors into play: historical distance (the gap between then and now) and the particular perspective from which the past is viewed. When we encounter history, he suggests, we engage with an entity other than ourselves, with a temporality of its own, and enter into something like a conversation, where we discover 'the other person's standpoint and horizon'.[28] But we do not just transpose ourselves onto this horizon because 'readers' have horizons of their own, complete with opinions (Gadamer calls them prejudices) that determine the position from which we meet history. The testing of such opinions constitutes the continual formation of the present in a loop that is itself dependent on the tradition we encounter from the past. Gadamer describes the situation as follows: 'There is no more an isolated horizon of the present in itself than there are historical horizons which have to be acquired. Rather, understanding is always the fusion of these horizons supposedly existing by themselves.'[29] We are, then, in a hermeneutic circle whereby we encounter ourselves in tradition and tradition in ourselves. The questions we ask of artefacts derive from our own horizon, but we also respond to questions generated by works themselves. Dahlhaus also talks of the past and present forming an indissoluble alloy, commenting, in the language of Gadamer, that 'the past is what has survived from the past, and hence is part and parcel of the present'.[30] The derivation is similarly obvious when he comments that the canon 'is transmitted by tradition: historians do not compile it so much as encounter it'.[31]

Jauss's critical modification of Gadamer's ideas can also be found in Dahlhaus, including the reproach that Gadamer universalizes to a general condition of art the classical humanist tradition, thereby applying the same criteria to both medieval and modern art.[32] In a similar, though not identical vein, we find Dahlhaus arguing that Gadamer's position is not appropriate for a good deal of twentieth-century music.[33] Taken a bit further, this objection threatens the fusion of horizons supposed by Gadamer, since the relationship between classical and modern ideas of music involves conflict and negation as well as transition. Pushed further still, it creates problems for

Dahlhaus as well as Gadamer, since it opens the prospect of competing horizons that cannot be reconciled with the notion of a single tradition. The consequences of multiple horizons can be pursued later; for now we can stay with overlapping themes in Dahlhaus and Jauss. The main idea shared with Jauss's influential essay 'Literary History as a Challenge to Literary Theory' occurs in a footnote in which he quotes from René Welleck's and Austin Warren's *Theory of Literature* the following sentences: 'Most leading histories of literature are either histories of civilization or collections of critical essays. One type is not a history of *art*; the other, not a *history* of art.'[34]

Derivatives of this idea, translated from a literary to a musicological context, occur abundantly in Dahlhaus's writings; indeed the prospect of a methodology that is both historical and musical is something of a preoccupation.[35] This fixation stems from a desire to avoid what Dahlhaus regards as the twin pitfalls of music history: dissolving music into a general social history or stringing together critical/analytical assessments of particular works with no linking historical thread. His remedy is to propose a methodology that would address the specifics of music while recognizing the impact of wider social processes, without collapsing one into the other. Jauss offers reception theory as a resource for such scholarship, since it is capable of theorizing the identity of a work by exploring the shifting interactions between the historical unfolding of its understanding and the changing horizons of its historical readers. Dahlhaus accepts this idea, and finds it assists in explaining why Bruckner's symphonies had their maximum impact in the 1920s, while the 1970s mark the high-water mark for Mahler's *oeuvre*.[36] But he is also aware that reception history opens space for interpretive horizons that may clash with those deriving from established tradition. The consequence is that Dahlhaus tends to uphold the structural claims of established masterpieces, while, in Hepokoski's words, admitting 'Jauss's ideas of reception history, social interaction, and the like only to those musical works whose status as art was disputed'.[37]

Alongside the hermeneutic currents in the Dahlhaus project runs a sharper dialogue, sometimes bristling into dispute, with Marxist methodology. Because Dahlhaus lived and worked in a divided Berlin, Marxism was a constant presence in his life. Major disputes erupted in West German universities during the 1960s and 1970s, with the most hard-line voices condemning the bourgeois tradition and Adorno's elitism. Dahlhaus's responses to these debates range from building on the subtlety of Adorno's ideas to lambasting Marxist orthodoxy for applying inappropriate criteria to art criticism. His most general complaint derives from his familiar insistence that music should not become absorbed into social history, especially one that understands the economic base to be the final, determining factor. This view of economic structure, he argues, 'implies that the tangled skein of technical, aesthetic, psychological, social and economic factors open to empirical investigation must always be interpreted on the basis of one single, unalterable hierarchy'.[38] He is also suspicious of ideology critique, since he feels that it tries to reduce historical analysis to underlying dogma, offering a choice between overt or covert bias. Such a suspicion, he comments, cannot be allayed; it must simply be borne.[39] This attitude is pragmatic to the extent that it resists the capacity of ideology critique to jam any project, even so Dahlhaus's stoicism is also rather defensive. Hepokoski is surely right to conclude that in such an environment Dahlhaus clearly felt the need both to shore up musicology as an academic discipline and to assert the German canon.[40]

Dahlhaus's comments on Adorno are scattered throughout his writings, offering analysis of particular problems but little in the way of thoroughgoing critique (a characteristic of his work, which can seem like a network of problems that avoids substantial statements). Some already familiar suspicions of Marxism resurface in this context, and inform the charge that Adorno imposes a preformed philosophy of history on music, rather than examining particular historical currents. The claim that social content is sedimented in the material form of music generates particular interest, since this is a way of tackling Dahlhaus's favourite problem: how to write a history of *art* (of, that is, specific works, and not merely of materials and forms) which is nonetheless a *history* of art (and not therefore a museum catalogue). Despite the lure of Adorno's theory of socialized material, Dahlhaus concludes that it is 'an attempt to overcome a contradiction which seems almost incapable of being bridged'. He adds that this may be an example of a problem that is more likely to become obsolete than to be solved;[41] a surprising judgement since the prospect of connecting music's technical and social dimensions remains of urgent interest.

Apart from practical concerns, Dahlhaus's suspicion of ideology critique stems from a desire to protect the Austro-German canon from sociological scrutiny, a propensity that renders him vulnerable to the kinds of criticism levelled at Gadamer. By talking of the canon as something one encounters, despite elsewhere contemplating the different rhythms of music history,[42] Dahlhaus speaks as the inhabitant of a particular canon with universal pretensions that tends to exclude those who prize other canons or ask other questions. Hepokoski describes the dilemma as follows: 'Dahlhaus's eleventh-hour attempt to stave off the collapse of the work-immanent integrity of Germanic "great works" seems fully, if grudgingly, aware of its own unfolding in a pluralistic, postmodern, and aesthetically entropic world'.[43] From studying historiography, aesthetics and reception history, Dahlhaus was well aware that music is embedded in a range of discourses that are not easily separated. But at the same time he was dedicated to a particular tradition, and was not prepared to let it collapse into sociology. His work is marked by a constant tension between unravelling and bolstering this tradition. If the result can at times seem something of an unproductive logjam, Dahlhaus's willingness to examine musicological methodology nevertheless has relevance beyond the limitations of his own horizon.

It would be foolish to attempt a synthesis of three figures as diverse as Kerman, Adorno and Dahlhaus, but from their differing perspectives we can identify themes and tensions that preoccupy current musicology. They have in common a concern with demonstrating how knowledge is dependent on often unstated assumptions that can be analysed, contested and possibly modified. The historical and sociological forces that construct the values of musical autonomy are another underlying interest, leaving as a residue the question of how the specific actuality of music can be understood alongside the social forms it embodies. A shared sense of crisis in the values enshrined in classical music is also central. We can ask, like Adorno, how these fare in a mechanized world, or contemplate how they adapt to different traditions and subjectivities. How music is affected by the global march of modernity and how it responds to and contributes to changing social environments are of course issues that are not restricted to the domain of classical music. Indeed all forms of music play a decisive role in the way people locate themselves in and between traditions. In short, music is one of the processes by which human subjects establish identities and generate affinities.

2 Discourses

Structuralism

The scientific turn Kerman describes in positivist and formalist musicology repudiates a more general musicology that is reluctant to declare its method or purpose, preferring to assume that one absorbs a particular mindset and learns the rules by association. Put another way, traditional musicology encloses music within a set of codes, but would prefer to transmit normative values than to acknowledge this frame. This model mysteriously blends biographies and music, inferring that composers operate in a historical continuum of evolving styles and create works that recognize standard forms, but deviate from them sufficiently to demonstrate originality. It assumes that musicians acquire knowledge of musical syntax by undertaking pastiche exercises and studying form, both imitative forms of transmission.

More conscious of its own procedures (though not without its own unstated assumptions), technical analysis seeks to understand music as a rigorous, logical process and is willing to apply tough methodology. Theory and analysis are the interdependent terms used to describe a field concerned both with establishing generalized procedures for understanding tonal and post-tonal music and with explanation of individual pieces. (Readers may wish to be reminded at this point that I take music theory to be a special branch of 'theory' as understood in more general parlance.) Normally analysis will take its lead from theoretical opinion, and theory will be reciprocally modified by the particular insights of analysis. With their shared belief in systematic explanation, they overturn some traditional views, while bolstering other conjectures by providing explanations in place of comfortable assumptions.

It is necessary to examine structuralism and poststructuralism as intellectual movements before considering how they touch on the more specialized aims of theory and analysis. Poststructuralism both breaks with structuralism and registers a continuous transformation that can be tracked through the writings of major figures associated with both movements such as Jacques Lacan, Michel Foucault and Roland Barthes.[1] For this reason, I shall present structuralist and poststructuralist topics sometimes in succession and sometimes simultaneously. And a further methodological distinction needs to be made, since one cannot discuss structuralism without touching on semiotics – the study of sign systems.[2] Semiotics derives from European and American roots, in particular from the work of the Swiss philologist Ferdinand de Saussure and the American philosopher Charles Pierce. Structuralism might be described as a particular historical branch of semiotics, mainly associated with a French intellectual movement. Beyond this definition, structuralism marks a wider movement of thought in the humanities and social sciences, characterized by the application of scientific rigour to areas that were accustomed to less stringent methodology. (Schenkerian analysis and set theory, for example, are not derived from French structuralism, but share its methodological assumptions.) Semiotics is also used in structuralist fashion to unearth deep codes, but it is equally a postmodern phenomenon that can be employed to celebrate diversity. Another way of saying this is that semiotics was reconfigured by the transition from structuralism to poststructuralism.

Structuralism, semiotics and poststructuralism all build on the observations made by Saussure in his *Course in General Linguistics*. Saussure was trained in philology, the accepted form of linguistics in his day, which examines the historical derivation and etymology of languages. His breakthrough was to analyse language as a sign system that constructs meaning, rather than simply reflecting it. Language as a signifying system that facilitates utterances he calls 'langue', but draws a distinction between langue and the individual utterances that provide instances of it, which he calls 'parole' (a distinction that has much in common with the division of duties between theory and analysis). He also argues that language can be studied synchronically, meaning that it can be examined at a particular historical moment (as a slice across time), as well as diachronically, that is, as it develops through time. His most celebrated claim concerns the constitution of the sign, which, he argues, is made up of two components, a signifier (a phonetic sound) and a signified (the concept to which it refers).

Importantly, signs are determined as much by what they are not as what they are: thus a 'dog' is dependent on not being a 'cat' or 'rabbit'. Finally, Saussure identifies paradigmatic and syntagmatic functions in language, observing a distinction between signs that can be substituted for one another and those that can form sequences of signs by association. 'Cat', for example, could be substituted for 'dog' in the sentence 'the dog is asleep', and either noun could participate in a sequence involving an article and verb. Taken all together, these claims convey language as a web in which meanings and functions are generated by networked relations.

These observations have continued to be of significance in the study of linguistics, but structuralism extends methods of linguistic analysis to other discourses. In a celebrated book Barthes turns his attention to advertising and fashion, maintaining that soap powder commercials, for instance, seek to overcome the contradiction of a light, frothy product with deep cleansing powers.[3] Claude Lévi-Strauss's less frivolous application of linguistic analysis to anthropology culminated in his four-volume *magnum opus*, *Introduction to a Science of Mythology* – a study of the indigenous myths of South and North America. He analyses this corpus synchronically, looking at how it works as a logical system rather than tracing its evolution. He also moves attention away from the narrative content of the myths and turns to the background codes that organize individual myths and the mythology as a system. These myths, it is claimed, reveal properties of the human mind; and when they are placed in families surface narratives can be peeled back to reveal abstract problems, often expressed in binary logic.

A section from volume 3 of the project (*The Origin of Table Manners*) entitled 'The Canoe Journey of the Sun and the Moon' provides some examples. Not surprisingly, this section deals with myths concerning the sun and the moon, who are sometimes depicted as paddler and steerer in a canoe. With two people in a canoe, the paddler and the steerer must sit at opposite ends to balance the vessel. This specification leads Lévi-Strauss to suggest that the opposition paddler/steerer is analogous to the binary pair sun/moon:

> The limited space in the canoe and the strict navigational rules tend to keep them at the *right distance* in relation to each other, together and separate at one and the same time, as the sun and the moon must be in order to avoid excessive daylight or excessive darkness which would scorch or rot the earth.[4]

The notion of scorching or rotting returns to a key theme of the tetralogy: that myths concerning cooking customs pertain to a conceptual ordering of the world. The binary pair cooked/rotten, it is contended, is analogous to the pair culture/nature, because raw food can either be culturally processed (cooked) or naturally processed (rotted).

Lévi-Strauss's analysis of myth provides a good example of systematic structuralism, but is also interesting in the present context because it draws significant parallels between myth and music. These comparisons are mainly found in 'Overture' and 'Finale' to the four volumes, while the chapter headings of the first volume, *The Raw and the Cooked*, are derived from musical forms. Overlaps between myth and music are sometimes pursued quite closely: it is suggested in the final volume, for example, that the myth of 'The Lewd Grandmother' adopts a fugal form.[5] The contention is that fugal structure is already present in myth, thus it is logical that the advent of fugue corresponds to the beginning of the modern age and the demise of mythic thought in the West.[6] Elsewhere, we learn that myth lies between music and speech (between syntax and semantics), and that both media share a special relationship to time: 'it is', Lévi-Strauss writes, 'as if music and mythology needed time only in order to deny it. Both, indeed, are instruments for the obliteration of time'; and both share the privilege of accessing 'inevitably unconscious truths'.[7]

This account of parallels between myth and music demonstrates a limited technical knowledge of music, but more important than this shortcoming is the notion that music as a syntactic, rather than semantic, art-form has a natural affinity with structuralist beliefs. Structuralism, it turns out, echoes many discourses prevalent in music theory that resonate with Eduard Hanslick's contention that music is about musical ideas.[8] In this respect, Lévi-Strauss draws on a nineteenth-century fascination with music's non-representational form as a metaphor for the structural rigour he brings to the study of myth. Similar origins also feed the mid-twentieth-century attempt to understand music objectively, which tried to find scientific, reductive language for notions of musical organicism that derive from the nineteenth century.

Affinities with the structuralist mindset are to be found in the mainly American attempt to transform the writings of Austrian music theorist Heinrich Schenker into a systematic theory of voice-leading in tonal music; an institutional assimilation that is roughly synchronous with the peak of structuralist activity. This is the project standardized for pedagogical purposes in Allen Forte's and Stephen Gilbert's *Introduction to Schenkerian Analysis*.[9] The graphic method strips surface detail down to linear and harmonic prolongation, eventually to a level in which the fundamental structure, derived from a linear and arpeggiated unfolding of the tonic triad, will emerge. The types of binary opposition made by Lévi-Strauss are not of central importance here (though the fundamental structure does try to reconcile the vertical with the horizontal), but an analytical methodology designed to demonstrate that surface detail is supported by deeper patterns affiliates easily with structuralism. This is even more the case when that underlying pattern is the overtone series (what Schenker called the chord of nature), since this underpinning naturalizes musical structure and removes it from historical contingencies. In this regard, the graphs are spatial abstractions that can be seen to freeze temporal structure into a single image. Having said this, however, it is nonetheless true that there is a certain tension between the timeless properties that underpin Schenkerian analysis and its capacity to show music unfolding through time, a characteristic that does not obviously tie in with the synchronic preoccupations of structuralism. The views of Schenker and his acolytes will shortly be re-examined; for present purposes it is more useful to pursue other manifestations of the structuralist theme in analysis.

In addition to codifying Schenker in a manner that is widely taught, Forte sought an equivalent to the fundamental structure in post-tonal music. Set theory, the result of these endeavours, seeks to identify, or create, a syntax that would govern the seemingly myriad surface patterns found in post-tonal music. Forte arranged combinations of pitch classes in prime form, which means that pitch classes (expressed as numerals) are packed in their closest ascending order. With large numbers of permutations reduced to this format, he was then able to produce an inventory of possible sets, against which the analyst can compare the actual sets, arranged in prime form, that are found in a particular piece. The aim of pitch-class set analysis, therefore, is to produce a list of intersecting sets, in the hope that some will emerge as especially significant because they contain the largest number of intersections. With its firm belief that surface phenomena are governed by underlying patterns, set theory is resolutely structuralist, and has been widely criticized for performing clinical autopsies on living organisms. Just as the structuralist analysis of myth turns away from narrative flow, so pitch-class analysis abandons the temporal unfolding of the music and looks for underlying similarities and differences.

Nevertheless, the process by which the analyst segments the music, or divides it into pitch classes, relies on rather conventional, even intuitive, understandings of texture, motivic working and phraseology, thereby diminishing the scientific precision of the tables it produces. The objective search for identity produces, paradoxically, a system (not unlike the codes of capitalist exchange) that cannot eradicate arbitrariness because one event can be made equivalent to another by a law external to its sensuous qualities. And this indeterminacy is reflected in the gap between the governing sets and the listening experience. Constructivist compositions are also afflicted by a comparable lacuna between their built-in systems and the sometimes arbitrary-sounding events perceived by the listener. This overlap is not particularly surprising since theory and compositional technique were closely linked in the mid-twentieth century, with the composer and theorist Milton Babbitt active in both camps. It is important to understand, however, that serial composition schemes generate structure rather than uncovering it in the manner of structuralism.[10]

Set theory is structuralist in its attempt to establish rules for identity and exclusion, but was not derived from mainstream structuralism. The same cannot, however, be said of the method of paradigmatic analysis pioneered by Nicolas Ruwet and Jean-Jacques Nattiez along explicity structuralist lines. Like the structuralist analysis of myth, this technique, which is particularly suited to monody, segments the diachronic process of the music into synchronic columns of equivalent events. It then searches for rules of identity and transformation between the isolated events. In doing so, it relies on an initial and perhaps intuitive appraisal of the music, but a thoroughgoing analysis such as Nattiez's account of Varèse's *Density 21.5* does, at least, have the merit of being explicit about its procedures.[11] A further advantage is that the technique can be applied to early and non-Western musics.

Less compelling, however, is Nattiez's beleagured belief that this type of analysis takes place on a neutral level (even if it is a hypothetical one), that is to say, a level uninfluenced by compositional intention or reception history. This idea is besieged by difficulties because it suggests that music and analytical methodology can somehow (if only temporarily) be removed from the discourses in which they are embedded. This is a typically structuralist problem, and we have seen that it is not difficult to find resemblances between structuralism and a range of analytical techniques willing to marginalize the network of discourses in which music participates in their search for underlying codes. The pioneering aspect of structuralism should not, however, be underestimated.

The scandalous side of structuralism is its readiness to examine venerated culture with a technical rigour that disrupts the transmission of established values and treats art as a rational construct. In this way analysis undermines cosy, humanist notions of art by locating quasi-automatic procedures in music. This impulse results in a conflict between what might be called democratic and technocratic tendencies. Taking the former first, we can see that despite Schenker's cult of the masterpiece and his elitism, the American adaptation of his theory has a magnanimous impulse, suggesting that it is not only experts who can understand how tonal masterpieces operate. Others, too, can also learn the technique and gain access to high art. Despite perpetuating an Austro-German canon, Schenkerism cuts through the mystique of the same music by showing how it functions. And despite this canonic devotion, one can analyse voice-leading in other repertoires such as popular music, though the notion of prolongation may require modification.[12] At a more general level, structuralism was an interdisciplinary movement that was not limited to the celebration of canonic artefacts, as Barthes's willingness to bridge the entrenched divide between literature and popular culture demonstrates. This impulse has the beneficial effect of releasing culture from stuffy traditions, but its darker side wrenches culture into a technological age in which subjectivity can, seemingly, be reduced to controlling patterns of signification. There is something disturbing about seeing a piece with personal associations by, say, Chopin, reduced to a graph with clinical efficiency. It corresponds to the alienating realization that our lives are determined by institutions that care little for our desires and hopes. The gap between the experience of music and its coding is felt most acutely in set theory, which is resolutely counter-intuitive.

Poststructuralism

The great arrogance that poststructuralism exposed was structuralism's belief that it could somehow transcend its own methodology and access fundamental principles. In the case of Lévi-Strauss, these fundamentals are supposed to be the abstract logic systems of the human mind that are apparent in musical forms such as the fugue. However, his suggestion that the advent of fugue is tied to the demise of myth in Western societies, thereby heralding the beginning of the modern age, fails to explain why the same structure should underpin an outdated historical form and its replacement. His assumption renders history a surface phenomenon that does not affect our deep perception of the world; and implies that fugue is a static form unaffected by varying historical contexts. The problem is symptomatic of a resolutely synchronic methodology that seeks to separate structure from cultural practice. Although rules of gender-coding and marriage, for example, clearly influence Lévi-Strauss's analytic segmentation, they take second place to more abstract themes, such as structural attempts to understand the binary divides encoded by nature and culture or sky and earth. However, just as the findings of set theory are more dependent on surface configurations than its claims suggest, so Lévi-Strauss's universalizing analysis is more indebted to contextual issues than he would care to admit. The problem is that a methodology willing to bracket certain experiences in favour of underyling principles starts to look like an ideology that will only countenance particular types of organization. Lévi-Strauss hopes to be above such issues by eliminating the subject, 'that unbearably spoilt child', he writes, 'who has occupied the philosophical scene for too long now, and prevented serious research through demanding exclusive attention'.[13] What this extraordinary statement amounts to is a belief that one can hold at bay the socio-historical influences that feed research methodology, and encounter knowledge in a pure form.

Not surprisingly, such abstract logic has received plenty of critical attention, because much that it would like to convey as rational and disinterested can be shown to represent prevailing technocratic interests. In the case of music, such interests are often not immediately evident, even so a mode of analysis that seeks an internal logic and is prepared to sacrifice detail and context to a vision of internal unity certainly depicts a chosen repertoire in a particular way. Often reluctant to examine timbre, intensity, gesture and sensuality, it represents a particular view of the musical subject – one that is self-determined and assured – while its logic represents a rationalist strand of modernity. With its commitment to structural principles, analysis is nevertheless often unwilling to examine the formations of subjectivity that propel its own endeavours. Yet when Schenker evokes the chord of nature to dehistoricize a particular repertoire, to separate it from a particular context, and to validate it by reference to timeless and universal laws, he is hypostasizing a canon associated with the rise of the bourgeois subject. Thus Schenkerian analysis is framed by a set of discourses about music, particularly the Beethoven reception history, but refuses to see the construction of its position and fails to understand the impact of its own beliefs. Analysis is always a form of subjectivity on the part of the theorist and the text, and a failure to understand this is a serious structuralist deficiency. Peter Dews, paraphrasing Lacan, makes an observation that can be equally well applied to analysis: 'the Lévi-Straussian and – in general – structuralist attempt to abolish the problem of the subject leads merely to the instatement of the symbolic system itself, self-enacting and self-perpetuating, as a kind of meta-subject'.[14]

One of the most repeated complaints made of analytical methodology is that it pretends to uphold the neutral values of a symbolic system instead of understanding itself as a shaping discourse. Like other methods of textual reading, it enacts a form of situated subjectivity. With this knowledge, musicology starts to look more like an ensemble of discourses of varying compatibility.[15] When one recognizes, for example, that background levels are intercrossed and situated by subjectivity, structural analysis can feed into a wider range of interpretive discourses. Hence the kind of opposition Pieter Van den Toorn defends between analysts who seek intimate knowledge of the object and those who offer views informed by gender studies or sociology need not exist,[16] for the simple reason that musical structures cannot be insulated from social pressures because they are already thoroughly socialized. The lesson to be drawn from structuralism is not that background codes are simply ideological projections, but that they are situated in a number of discourses and the claims made for them should be open to scrutiny.[17] The point is not that underlying mental and physiological operations do not exist, but that they are encountered in historically and culturally specific ways. Saying this does not automatically offer history as a candidate for the 'ultimate reality or source of truth', mirroring structuralism's totalizing tendencies, since history, too, can be read as a construction, as something to be challenged and scrutinized.[18]

A willingness to bypass the subject and a reluctance to reflect on the historical location of its own discourses are structuralist problems that remain endemic to poststructuralism. But before examining these issues and looking further at the impact of poststructuralism on analytical theory, it is worth pursuing poststructuralism's transformation and critique of structuralism in more general terms, noting en route its consequences for Lévi-Strauss's views on music. We have already touched on poststructuralist themes in observing Lèvi-Strauss's reliance on music as a metaphor that supplements his supposedly self-contained analysis of myth, and in observing Schenker's dependence on a natural authority, whether tonal, religious or national. Poststructuralism challenges the idea that one can step behind a discourse to examine its underlying codes, and deconstruction might be described as a sub-discipline of poststructuralism.

Deconstruction is not a methodology one learns and then applies to texts, but it does pursue certain themes, such as the rhetorical strategies used in writing and the dependency of ideas on the medium in which they are expressed, that enable it to quarry the conflicting patterns of signification at work in texts. By text it alludes to a wider range of discourses than just literature, and much of its political significance lies in a willingness to read institutions as text and to examine the mechanisms by which they consolidate meaning. It might, for example, read a literary text as philosophy, looking for its conceptual apparatus, or examine the rhetorical strategies pursued in a philosophical treatise, refusing to accept that one genre is about objective thought and the other about creative expression. Clearly, then, deconstruction has a different view of text, or more properly textuality, than the positivist methodologies discussed in Chapter 1. For poststructuralism, a text is not an object with clearly defined boundaries that fix meaning, but an ensemble of discourses.

In his famous *Of Grammatology*, Jacques Derrida examines what he calls a 'logocentric' tendency across a diverse range of writers, including Lévi-Strauss, Saussure and Jean-Jacques Rousseau, who all, according to traditional readings, consider that writing is a substitute, or supplement, to speech: that the codes of language are somehow stabilized by the presence of a speaker. Crucially, Derrida does not simply disagree with this opinion or offer an alternative; instead he pulls strands from the texts that undercut this thesis. By showing how speech is dependent on its supplement, he demonstrates that the supplement is somehow always there and cannot therefore be excluded by an origin since it is already at the origin. Furthermore, he does not attempt to step out of this conundrum or to substitute writing for speeech; rather he shows how the one is dependent on the other, that is, how the two terms differ and defer to each other in a space he calls *différance*.

As an example, we can examine Derrida's deconstruction of a passage from Lévi-Strauss's *Tristes tropiques*.[19] The anthropologist presents the speech/writing theme in terms of a nature/culture opposition, arguing that the introduction of writing to a particular tribe is linked to the beginning of social division. Derrida's reading draws another conclusion: that division, indeed violence, was already evident in the society, that it was never entirely consistent with itself because the idea of a supplement that would open difference in the social order was always there. He also finds a manifestation of such logocentricism in Rousseau's preference for the Italian music of his time, with its melodic emphasis, over what he views as the contrived artificiality of French music as embodied in the harmonic theory of Jean-Philippe Rameau.[20] The pattern is familiar: melody, in standard readings of Rousseau, embodies the presence of human emotions, while harmony depletes this plenitude by introducing articulation. Uncovering another strand in the text, Derrida demonstrates that singing itself already involves articulation and cannot, therefore, be identical with expression because the supplement of harmony is already there.

Rousseau's discussion of music is also used by Paul De Man in a debate with Derrida in which he claimed that the counter-discourse in Rousseau was a deliberate textual strategy.[21] Rousseau may appear to favour melody for its plenitude, De Man argues, but there is also a voice in the argument that values the diachronic tendencies of melody over the synchronic qualities of harmony. This voice recognizes that even repetition takes place in time and hence cannot be self-identical, consequently harmony cannot be released from this logic, though it appears to cohere in a single moment.

That both writers find two strands in Rousseau is of more importance than their disagreements about textual strategy; furthermore, it is highly significant that music is used as the medium for this exchange. The idea lodged in Rousseau's text – intentionally according to De Man, unintentionally according to Derrida – that music as a temporal medium cannot be identical with itself, is also of significance for Lévi-Strauss's dependence on music as a metaphor. If the structural analysis of myth is able to access the neat, binary operations of the human mind, one might ask, why should its results need the metaphor of music? The implication is that there is a gap between the myths and the claims made for them that is plugged by reference to music. Moreover, if deconstruction shows that Lévi-Strauss's assessment of music as the structuralist medium *par excellence* is based on an untenable metaphor, De Man gives the muse a comparable status within poststructuralist discourse. For if from the structuralist viewpoint music's temporality freezes over into synchronic pattern, then from the poststructuralist perspective, music embodies the non-coincidence of temporality because it is all relationship. Ironically, therefore, De Man comes close to essentializing music, and is more indebted to the nineteenth-century idea of music as pure form than he might care to admit.

Lévi-Strauss and De Man are dealing here more with what we might call the idea of music than actual musical practices, but the organic metaphors they both pursue (though with different agendas) are also prevalent in the disciplinary measures applied to existing music.[22] There is, therefore, a parallel to be made between the way that nineteenth-century music aesthetics found a quasi-scientific voice in Lévi-Strauss, and the way that Schenker's views on organicism hardened into 'objectivity' as they became institutionalized in the twentieth century. Some of Schenker's nationalist and religious beliefs proved embarrassing and dropped off in this transition, while others such as the creed of autonomy hardened. The Americanization of Schenker that I am discussing here creates a certain confusion since its scientific zeal is not always compatible with the nineteenth-century ideas that pervade Schenker's own writings.[23] For this reason, it is necessary to distinguish Schenkerism from Schenker's own writings because recent work has reversed some of the narrowing of his theory by placing it within the interpretive practice of its time.[24] Schenker cannot, however, be absolved of all responsibility for later readings of his theory since an underlying metaphysics, or presence as Derrida would call it, remains stubbornly present in later manifestations. The fundamental structure – however technically it is presented – is rooted in the idea that the chord of nature underpins tonal masterpieces.

It is easy to insert Derridean levers here. If the tonic triad is identical with itself, one might enquire, why should music move to the dominant in order to confirm the tonic? Does this model of departure and return not indicate that there is some lack in the tonic that requires a supplement? Furthermore, does the relational scheme of levels found in Schenkerian analysis not suggest more a pattern of deferment than absolute identity? And finally, does structural unfolding not prove surprisingly dependent on the specifics of surface detail that are stripped away in analytical reduction? Such questions do not suggest that it is meaningless to talk of middleground voice-leading, only that strong patterns of essential structure cannot be cleanly shaven of marginal detail. If deconstruction problematizes Schenkerian ideas of textual closure and indicates that the spatial metaphor of the fundamental structure is untenable, it does not deny that voice-leading offers insights into Schenker's chosen repertoire. It suggests, rather, that music comprises a network of signifying codes that is unlikely to be harnessed by a single configuration. Voice-leading graphs, when released from dogma, can bring to attention conflicting or ambiguous processes in music and need not marginalize moments that refuse to be contained by the whole form.

It might be concluded from the above discussion that critical theory has much to say about music theory, but little to say about music itself. This, however, is precisely the type of distinction that post-structuralism challenges, by questioning whether there is a music outside the ways in which we 'read' or hear it. Nevertheless, deconstructive themes can also be located in case studies. Rose Rosengard Subotnik's discussion of Chopin's A major Prelude, Op. 28 No. 7, for example, focuses on the climactic F sharp seventh chord in bar 12 (see Ex. 1).[25] The chord is surprising in a number of ways: its function as a climax is assured by occupying the highest register in the music and by the crescendo approach, yet it converts the preceding tonic A major harmony into the dominant of B minor. It signifies closure, therefore, while simultaneously destabilizing the tonic that would provide such safety. This analysis is restricted to harmonic functions, however the supplemental quality of this moment is also apparent when the voice-leading is graphed according to Schenkerian principles. Craig Ayrey's middleground graph shows the event as subsidiary to the unfolding of the fundamental line, thereby indicating it is not required for the voice-leading to achieve satisfactory closure, despite the event asserting itself as the climax through its cadential characteristics and registral displacement. As both climax and supplement, the seventh chord reveals the fundamental line to be complete, yet insufficient.[26]

Texts

So far we have looked at music as a metaphor for structural coherence and examined the disciplinary embodiment of that idea in music theory, noting the dependence of both views on organicist aesthetics.

Ex. 1

Both approaches merge when Lévi-Strauss names Wagner as 'the undeniable originator of the structural analysis of myths', adding 'it is a profoundly significant fact that the analysis was made, in the first instance, in *music*'.[27] By mentioning *The Ring*, Lévi-Strauss touches on a project that really does have affinities with his own interweaving of music and myth, and yet Wagner's multitextual sensibility hardly supports the narrowly structural view of music that Lévi-Strauss advocates. It is scarcely a coincidence that Wagner was the main opponent to the kind of theory put forward by Hanslick that Lévi-Strauss's argument otherwise resembles. The paradox is that Wagner's handling of music and myth supports parallels with aspects of Lévi-Strauss's analysis of myth, but undercuts his views on the structural purity of music since it stands opposed to the aesthetics of absolute music.

Let us take the parallels first. Catherine Clément points out that *The Ring* does indeed break myths down into bundles of relationships, in structuralist fashion, that are not derived from its narrative unfolding. She gives an example:

> Siegmund is killed by Wotan's spear/Siegfried breaks Wotan's spear; Wotan sends Brünnhilde to sleep and surrounds her with flames/ Brünnhilde procures eternal rest for Wotan and lights the funeral pyre. In both cases the events resemble and thwart one another, the second both annulling and repeating the first. To see these correlations, one must stop listening to the narrative in chronological order and leap backward, anachronistically.[28]

If one event can be substituted for another, Clément is saying, then occurrences are defined more by their function than by their narrative significance, and if paradigmatic events can be endlessly replaced and thus alter the sequence of the narrative, then it is not surprising that the story of *The Ring* is varied every time it is told.[29] Nor is this process limited to the mythic narration, since the leitmotifs also form bundles of relations (Dahlhaus calls them webs),[30] which is why Wagner resists interpretation in the frame of symphonic motivic working. The problem for structuralism is that these narrative inconsistencies create a certain indeterminacy in the patterns of signification that is not eradicated at a deeper level. The music and words function like a giant web, where one discourse refers to another without the prospect of closure. In this way Wagner's multitextual aesthetic draws attention to the codes that frame music, and hence, unwittingly, to the processes by which textual meaning is negotiated. Unlike Lévi-Strauss's formalist view of music, Wagner textualizes music.

Prompted by this observation, we can explore further the distinction poststructuralism makes between work and text. Barthes describes the work as an object whose signification is closed by the imprint of its author, and comments 'there is now the requirement of a new object, obtained by the sliding or overturning of former categories'.[31] This new object is intertextual: held between other texts, it is a multi-dimensional space, a methodological field, in which discourses circulate. When text is understood in this way, authorial control is reduced and the immanent meaning of a text becomes less distinguishable from what readers make of it. These thoughts, which have become standard for poststructuralism, show Barthes the structuralist becoming Barthes the poststructuralist, acutely aware that there are no meta-codes with which to stabilize interpretation. Originality and authority cannot be attributed solely to the text and derivation and subservience entirely to the critic, since both produce texts that interact and signify. The work of the psychoanalyst Lacan, for example, is a set of unconventional readings of Freud.

The power of the reader will be explored further in the next chapter, but for now I want to look at the idea of textuality. Just as the boundary between text and reader is permeable, Barthes suggests, so is the boundary between text and text, since it is crossed by multiple codes. This is true in the traditional sense of music history, which unfolds like a narrative, with works and composers influencing each other. It is also true in a more literal sense of intertextuality where one piece alludes to or quotes from another: Schumann's Op. 17 Fantasy for piano, for example, includes a quotation from Beethoven's song cycle *An die ferne Geliebte* (*To the Distant Beloved*), a gesture that cannot be attributed entirely to an internal logic. Genre is also intertextual, with music tacitly referencing other examples in the field, as demonstrated by the dialogue between Mozart and Haydn in their string quartet output. What all this points to is that music is thoroughly contextualized, hence it is difficult, if not impossible, rigidly to control the contexts in which it is interpreted.

What does all this mean for musicology and for performance conventions based on the authority of the score? Poststructuralism indicates that there is not a 'music itself' that can be separated from the discourses or media associated with it, and this point extends right into the notation of the medium. Notation is not a neutral device that transparently records ideas formulated independently of it; it is an intrinsic part of the message and impacts on the ways in which musicians conceive and perceive music. The notation of a Beethoven symphony, for example, specifies pitch quite accurately, hence it is no coincidence that analysis attends to this dimension. However, it is less attuned to timbre and orchestral balance, which are determined largely by performance traditions, and therefore subject to the vagaries of transmission. True, not all music is notated, but all music can be recorded and replayed, that is to say, mediated by a process dependent not only on the type and placing of equipment but also on editorial decisions made in the studio.[32] In the case of electronic and computer music, technology is intimately linked both to the creative process and to the method of dissemination, even when the inbuilt tendencies of software are resisted.

Notation is not just a set of conventions essential to the medium, it also marks an authorial presence. There are parallels here with the art market where signature propels value, with fortunes sometimes resting on the veracity of a painter's squiggle because it confers the uniqueness of the object and the presence of the artist. As a performing art, music is not as dependent on signature as the visual arts, but its authority is nevertheless crucial to the ways in which music is valued and studied. Manuscripts are prized for the composer's inferred presence, which imparts a mechanism for controlling the signification of the text, and studied for information they might yield on his (it usually is) intentions. Reference to a manuscript often attempts to invoke authorial authority over the reception history that has accrued to the work, even though an autograph score depicts an intention at a particular time, not absolute purpose. Furthermore, we know that composers change their ideas about works, as the different speeds at which Stravinsky conducted *The Rite of Spring* demonstrates. Pierre Boulez is forever reworking his music, and the recent orchestration of some early piano pieces, *Notations*, clearly indicates how his ideas have expanded. In the case, moreover, of a pianist-composer such as Chopin, who would alter a score in performance, it is impossible to establish a definitive manuscript.[33]

But if composers change their minds, they are also often keen to establish their intentions, whatever the difficulties; in fact the modernist tendency to convey greater detail in scores runs hand in hand with the musicological championing of authorial design. Look at the detailed instructions in Mahler's scores, which include reminders to conductors of previous markings, depicting a desire for authorial sovereignty over what the composer knows to be the conditions of performance. Such controlling procedures tend, however, to become enmeshed in the discourses they seek to master. By inviting close scrutiny of a manuscript, they risk revealing it to be a construction, not an inviolable utterance.

Allied to the notion of a definitive score is the authenticity movement's attempts to fix interpretative practice. Discounting developments in instrument technology and performance convention, its quarry is the music as it would have been heard in its time, reinvented by using original instruments and whatever accounts of performances are to hand. In one sense, this chase appears to be a misguided attempt to find a source for music and imbue it with presence; an undertaking that is likely to result in a messy attempt to privilege one discourse over others by imposing a modern fetish of purity on a wide range of music. In another sense, it is a form of resistance to a performing tradition that in the twentieth century has become homogenized and standardized. The authenticity movement, then, is caught up in a paradoxical attempt to find an origin that would control the signifying practices of performers and other interpreters, but is reluctant to examine its own 'origin' as a reaction to modernity and slow to value its own creative dynamic.

Less wary of modern institutions, the cult of the conductor is also prey to the logic of presence. Conductors undoubtedly execute necessary functions in keeping performances of large nineteenth-century scores afloat, but on a less practical plane they also invoke, through a series of ritualized expressions and gestures, the presence of the composer – the person who channels and controls the signification of the music. The conductor, then, can be understood as a supplement in Derrida's sense: the music is complete without him, but by adding to this completion he indicates an insufficiency. He is, we are to believe, someone in direct contact with lofty musical ideals that are unleashed at the flick of a stick, yet because they are mediated through him they are more contingent than they might otherwise seem. His authority derives from the reception history of a particular canon and from the nineteenth-century organization of the orchestra as a labour force under the control of a manager. The maestro is the managing director in total control, but one who experiences deep sentiments and has a workforce that will respond to his every whim. Despite this authority, he indicates that music does not just speak; it requires interpretation, and is therefore not a fixed code but depends on the rhetoric of performance to convey meaning. This condition amounts to more than the obvious truth that one needs an orchestra to perform a symphony: it means that the music must be brought to life. Performance, therefore, is a special kind of active reading, whether it derives from a written text or a set of assimilated codes (an improvisation).

The above discussion shows that scores cannot be detached from their textual procedures, and this observation has ramifications for most strands of musicology. Comparable issues are alive in the compositional passage from serialism to post-serialism. Barthes himself notes the text is like a post-serial score in which the performer is asked to complete the composition. The musical equivalent to the open text was pioneered by Karlheinz Stockhausen in *Klavierstück XI* and by Boulez in his Third Piano Sonata. In both these pieces the performer is given choices on how to proceed from one section to the next, though Boulez tries to retain authorial control: for him the sequences are meant to represent properties of the serial permutations, and he likens the choices to those made on a street map where one's freedom is curtailed by the existing streets. In these scores the performer becomes a reader (of maps), though the role of the listener is not greatly enhanced; unless of course she has an agenda of her own aside from modernist language games. John Cage's indeterminate scores are more obviously textual in their reduction of control over sounds, but do not always grant performers and listeners active roles as constructors of meaning. In this sense, his works are structuralist artefacts controlled by anonymous, steering mechanisms. The other side of the coin is that they create a situation to be interpreted, and subjectivity does, albeit tacitly, play an increasing role in Cage's later work. It is certainly an active ingredient for a post-Cage experimental composer such as the American Pauline Oliveros, who attempts to break down the distinction between audience and performers and encourages participants to construct events from their own experiences.[34]

It is worth dwelling for a moment on the relationship between modernist art and poststructuralism, particularly deconstruction, despite the latter's unwillingness to situate itself in relation to the discourses of modernity, which might look suspiciously like an origin. Derrida's interest in figures such as Stéphane Mallarmé and Antonin Artaud, and the regard for him across a broad swathe of cultural criticism, suggest that deconstruction has strong links with modernism. Artistic practices experienced a crisis in traditional organicist aesthetics, and consequently became self-reflexive. Deconstruction extends this impulse into criticism, blurring the divide between text and critic. In the aftermath of high modernism, some would argue that its critical impetus has been transferred into theory, where much creative contemporary aesthetic practice is to be found. And theory, of course, extends the impact of modernist and postmodernist experience to a wide range of culture.

One of the most widely influential themes to emerge from poststructuralism is the idea that one can never limit the context in which a text might be interpreted. Before expanding on this statement, it is necessary to know something of the linguistic debates from which the idea arose. The distinction linguists make between constative and performative draws attention to the gap between the intended meaning of a statement (constative) and the effect it has (performative). Because one can never completely determine the context in which language operates, advocates of the performative argue, one can never completely determine its outcome. Looking at language in this way is implicit in most of Derrida's work, but becomes explicit in a now famous encounter with John Searle's brand of Anglo-American linguistic philosophy.[35] Derrida takes issue with Searle's attempt to contain the performative (as presented in J.L. Austin's *How to Do Things with Words*) by demoting it from a constituent feature of language to a special instance. Derrida's point is that the performative dimension cannot be contained because one can always envisage a context, such as a joke or a play, in which the intention of a statement might change.[36] The gap between intention and result is a familiar idea. When a composer analyses music by someone else, for instance, he often tells us more about his own preoccupations than about the score in question. Boulez's analysis of *The Rite of Spring* furnishes an example, since his focus on internal structural features of the music has much to do with his own integral serialist thinking of the time.[37]

A related theme that emerges from discussions of the performative is the idea that we should consider not only what texts mean but what they do, since discourses do not just reflect or encode ideas that come from elsewhere, they help to create them. And this is equally true of music and musicology. Nineteenth-century music is not just about the bourgeois subject, it helps to create that subject; similarly musicology is not just about music, it partly brings it into being. Put like this, music and musicology share characteristics of all discourses, so the much-discussed gap between the referential quality of language and the non-referential qualities of music becomes less significant.[38]

Nevertheless, performative hazards are more evident in language than in music. The widely practised political art of spin doctoring, for example, is about creating events, and thus a particular reception, through language that can be creative, but can also be misleading and manipulative, especially when one party is privy to more information than another. Such issues become crucial when one hears conflicting reports of a serious event such as a massacre. Clearly in this instance, the reporting does not create the event, and one would want to separate evidence of what took place from propaganda. Such transparency is more an ideal than an actuality, but accurate communication does depend on minimizing performative twisting. Even though music and musicology do not usually face responsibilities of such magnitude, words can undoubtedly be set with a certain spin on them. And the distrust of modernism shown by Nazi and Soviet regimes clearly shows that what music does is of political interest. The very fact that modernism proved to be a battleground for conflicting ideologies is itself proof that music does not dwell outside such polemics.

Poststructuralism can be performatively pulled in different directions by various commentators, as befits a theory that places emphasis on the reader. Focusing on Derrida, two main responses are prevalent, which highlight different areas of his work. One, represented by Christopher Norris, regards it as a strict exposure of the Enlightenment's blind spots and unexamined assumptions, yet one which retains faith with the project of modernity: he argues that 'Derrida's writings are always aimed at locating the stress-points or moments of self-contestation where texts come up against the ineluctable limits of their own ideological project.'[39] The other reading, pursued by Richard Rorty, emphasizes Derrida's work on rhetoric and the performative, often to justify pluralist interpretation and anti-foundationalism. A variant on the second position – and Jürgen Habermas is the primary exponent of this stance – is taken by those who value transparent communication and regret Derrida's attempts to extend textual indeterminacy beyond the realm of literature. All of these readings can claim some justification, since Derrida's writings range from the philosophically serious to the rhetorically playful; but his later work engages with politics and history and he clearly wishes to disassociate himself from those who view deconstruction as concerned exclusively with the free play of language in isolation from more worldly issues. In his words:

> It [the text] does not suspend reference – to history, to reality, to being, and especially not to the other, since to say of history, of the world, of reality, that they always appear in an experience, hence in a movement of interpretation which contextualizes them according to a network of differences and hence of referral to the other, is surely to recall that alterity (difference) is irreducible. *Différance* is reference and vice versa.[40]

Clearly, then, Derrida wants us to know that textual interpretation is a very worldly activity.

Poststructuralism offers a powerful critique of music's institutions and methodologies, and does much to bring musicology into general humanities discourses, preventing perception of it as an isolated discipline with its own narrow concerns. It highlights the textual qualities of music and its discourses, demonstrating just how interdependent they are. Even within the field of music criticism, however, poststructuralism offers differing possibilities: it can be seen to encourage the view that musical discourses are just clever rhetorical strategies, or it can be used as a tool to interrogate those strategies and their assumptions. When the second interpretation prevails, poststructuralism provides tools to identify the ideological assumptions built into naturalized outlooks. By showing texts to be constructions, poststructuralism does much to shake analytical tenets of abstraction and organicism, and encourages analysts to examine just what they think they are discovering in music. More broadly, poststructuralism punctures the arrogance of structuralism by showing how its God's-eye view is entangled in linguistic strategies. This deflation has wide-ranging significance because it empowers voices that are marginalized by discourses and institutions seeking a dominant interpretation. Poststructuralist discourses can be as anonymous and ahistorical as structuralist codes, but they need not be because the emphasis on the reader as a constructor of texts heralds, potentially, the return of the subject. The subject returns not as a diligent reader of authorial intentions, but as an active voice. The next chapter will explore the consequences of reading from various subject positions, but before this we can turn to recent ideas on musical semantics.

Semantics

Both structuralism and poststructuralism have exerted influences on the literary field of narratology, which has been thoroughly mined by recent searches for musical meaning. We saw in the structural analysis of myth how Lévi-Strauss distinguishes the events that take place in a myth from the narrative presentation of them, and how his analytical technique, designed to show the myths as a logical language, rearranges events into bundles that are related to each other, usually through binary opposition. In short, he makes a distinction between a sequence of events and the discourse that presents them; and this separation is shared by all theories of narrative (though sometimes one has to search for it). When it is mapped onto music one quickly runs into debates about its non-referential nature. For Nattiez, music can never be a narrative – a linked series of events – in the way that language can, since talk of narrative in music can only be metaphorical. By adopting a 'narrative frame of mind', he maintains, we can map a musical scheme onto an imagined succession of events, and the linearity of musical occurrences encourages us to draw analogies with the linearity of linguistic narratives.[41] His point is that narrative cannot be in the music; it can only be a metaphorical construct on the part of the listener. This conclusion falls victim to a neat divide between music and discourse, failing to understand that all musicology actively shapes our perception, performance and creation of music. Thus when we speak of narrative in music, the situation is not different from general issues of meaning in music, which stem from an intersection of music and discourse, and are not entirely located in either. To put this another way, modifying Derrida's language, meaning is neither inside nor outside the music. It is true, however, that some readings will be more text- or reader-based than others; and strong narrative readings do fall into the latter category, requiring a good deal of work from the listener.

Modern ideas on music and discourse enable us to renegotiate debates of the nineteenth century about programme versus absolute music. The extremes are represented, firstly, by Hanslick's view that absolute music is about nothing but itself and, secondly, by Berlioz's meticulous attempts to translate programmes into sound and to construct programmes for existing music.[42] Both writers fail to understand how much their own discourses contribute to the music they discuss and, in Berlioz's case, create. Some music is of course more susceptible to a narrative frame of mind, and the programme associated with the *Symphonie fantastique* positively encourages it. Music, unlike film, cannot represent events, but it can allude to them semiotically, as a film might do, through 'angles' and 'inserts', leaving the listener to complete the rest of the event.[43] Anthony Newcomb has suggested that:

> The narrative quality in Mahler's music emerges most powerfully from the intersection of formal paradigm, thematic recurrence, and . . . plot archetype – that is to say, various standard configurations of actions or intentions, configurations that are a fundamental part of our vocabulary for interpreting the design and intention of human action and its simulacrum, narrative.[44]

Such archetypes are associated with a historically defined group in which Beethoven's Third, Fifth and Ninth Symphonies serve as anchor points, with A.B. Marx's heroic programme for the *Eroica* functioning as the locus classicus of narrative readings.[45] The plot of temporal resolution is found not only in the four-movement sonata, but also in the dynamic single-movement sonata form, whose formal plan might be described as embodying a situation that is developed and returned to with renewed insight.

Closely related to conceptions of the bourgeois subject who triumphs over adversity, this archetype suggests a heroic character who departs from home, makes his way in the world and returns with maturity; a type of narrative that became explicit in Liszt's and Strauss's tone poems, most obviously in the latter's *Ein Heldenleben* (*A Hero's Life*). Such overtly programmatic compositions court hostility because bonding instrumental music to narrative content insinuates that the symphonic tradition may be less abstract than custom decrees. Some argue that this kind of purposive narrative embodies a defensive subject formation, typically male, that seeks to subjugate nature and extraneous impulses.[46] There is evidence to support such readings, but it should be remembered that music can also turn archetypes towards experiences they would normally exclude – even the relentless energy of the first movement of Beethoven's Fifth is interrupted by the 'reflective' oboe cadenza at the recapitulation. Narrative readings interact with the complex grid of social, cultural and material codes that contribute to the construction of subjectivity in music. Impossible to prove, they are gambits, bridging the gap between discourse and object, whose success depends on their power to convince.[47]

Analogies between musical processes and a sequence of events is one way of understanding music as narrative. Another, not necessarily incompatible approach, is to look for moments when the music becomes reflexive, or somehow 'conscious' of its own narrative strategy. Carolyn Abbate's study of nineteenth-century musical narrative employs this narrow approach and is mainly concerned with operatic narrative and programme music because, for her, music narrates only rarely.[48] She does, however, find narrative moments in instrumental music and these act in almost deconstructive manner: self-consciously out of place in a dynamic form, they are voices from outside that enact their own performance. The theme Mahler marked 'Gesang' (song) in the first movement (*Todtenfeier*) of his Second Symphony provides an instance of such localized narrative, creating instability at each entry, she argues, because 'with the "Gesang" there is not merely a musical *contrast*, but a registral shift to musical discourse that signals a *singer* and a *song*'.[49]

Adorno's study of Mahler also notices the effects of music with narrative associations on a symphonic plot. He hears the second subject in the first movement of the Fourth Symphony as 'an instrumental song far too self-sufficient for a sonata as such',[50] and notes a gap in the transition from the first to second subject, despite the normal sonata logic. Robert Samuels has provided the analysis implied by Adorno's comments, heeding the cleft between this perception and what analytical techniques tell us about the music. 'Where a Schenkerian reduction would find no problem at all', Samuels comments, 'Adorno hears an intertextual problem: in fact, the problem of the unproblematic nature of this transition.'[51] But Adorno also hears narrative reflexivity on a larger scale in Mahler, commenting, in a remark that has become a touchstone for work on musical narrative, that [the] 'music recites itself, is its own content, narrates without narrative'.[52] His idea rests on a distinction, or fissure, between the narrative flow of the music and its formal events: that is to say, the music is not identical with itself because it comments, reflexively, on its own strategies. Certain types of material such as theme, transition and development, he suggests, move with the flow of the music, but are not overdetermined by it because they have lives of their own. Mahler's willingness to cast the symphony as a story, as something that was once a possibility, is for Adorno an index of a socio-historical crisis in the symphony, hence in the idea of the self-determining bourgeois subject. Consequently Mahler's narrativizing plays for higher stakes than textual ambiguity: in its self-awareness music encounters the world.

So far, we have talked about reading narrative in instrumental music, yet music's relation to narrative can be more direct: it can function alongside it, or even inside it, to use a distinction made by film theorists, who describe music that is part of the represented scene (often listened to or performed by the characters) as diegetic, and music outside this frame (usually on a sound track) as non-diegetic. The employment of music in film and TV relies on audience familiarity with semiotic codes that reinforce or diverge from screen images, which of course have their own semiotic repertoire. Classical music as a genre carries the general codes 'posh', 'expensive' or 'privileged', though romantic styles have escaped from classical associations to become familiar resources for film music, often found in John Williams's scores for action films such as *Superman* and *Star Wars*. Popular music is frequently used more specifically to establish a certain peer group identity. But categories are not stable, since film music is a major catalyst in breaking down classical/popular distinctions.

Just such a fusion is discussed by Philip Tagg in a pioneering semiotic analysis of the 1970s detective series *Kojak*. Tagg breaks the score down into various musemes (units of meaning), which include the virile heroism of the horn theme and the aggressive atmosphere of a North American inner city (basses, cellos and electric bass). He tests his hypothesis of the horn theme against various other triadic horn themes, such as Siegfried's horn call from Wagner's *Ring*, the opening statement of Strauss's *Ein Heldenleben* and the unison horn motif from the same composer's *Don Juan* (which also returns in *Ein Heldenleben*).[53] These themes certainly provide precedents for Tagg's claim, though a general audience is more likely dimly to associate them with an archetype than to know the scores he cites. Tagg's analysis shows how the semiotic associations of the music interact with and influence screen images, instead of simply reflecting them. Anyone doubting that music carries these associations need only to imagine the *Kojak* theme introducing BBC Radio Four's *Gardeners' Question Time*.

To understand the narrative expectations these associations carry, we can turn to the modern thriller, for which *Kojak* serves as a precursor. The standard plot for this film genre is an impaired version of the heroic struggle over adversity, characteristic of much nineteenth-century culture, translated into a contemporary urban setting. The archetypal figure for such a plot is the maverick cop, alienated by bureaucracy but admired by his colleagues for his 'hands on' approach to crime. When pursuing a particularly tough criminal, or criminal association, he tracks his prey through unconventional means. After the restoration of order, he is reunited with the authorities who cannot deny the effectiveness of his individualistic ways. The genre will appeal, typically, to a male viewer trapped by his paper-shuffling job, who resents his employers yet wants to win their approval.

The narrative is, of course, a fantasy: no organization would tolerate such maverick behaviour, let alone reward it. The rugged individualism of the cop, which mimes the criminal's disregard for the law, is incompatible with an administered society. *Kojak*-type music, then, contains a contradiction. On the one hand, it registers a call for an impaired subjectivity to be something else, but the alternative it offers is itself a repressed form of subjectivity that hopes to control others while also seeking approval. As Hayden White observes, narrative is perhaps the principal instrument for the dissemination of ideology in the modern world, since people are taught to absorb narratives that obscure analysis of their social situation by portraying illusory images of it. In his words: 'Ideologies are apprehended as generic class- or group-fantasies addressed to the imaginary dimensions of consciousness where infantile dreams of individual wholeness, presence and autonomy operate as compensatory reactions to the actual, severed and alienating conditions of social existence.'[54] As we shall see, such ideologies play important roles in popular music, especially in masculinist genres such as heavy metal.

Music is awash with identities and images offered in concoctions of varying ideological strength and in a variety of media such as song, opera and video (which are considered in the next two chapters). As the above discussion of narrative ideology suggests, discourses shape and modify identity, yet poststructuralism, like structuralism, is prone to underplay the importance of identity. 'The reader', Barthes once observed, 'is without history, biography, psychology; he is simply that *someone* who holds together in a single field all those traces by which the written text is constituted.'[55] This is not a tenable position, since it suggests that readers (and authors) are little more than nodal points in language, while simultaneously dismantling the work concept so as to empower readers as active constructors of meaning. In response to this dilemma theories of reading – and feminism is important in this regard – tend to promote the situated reader, thereby bringing the subject back into poststructuralism. After all, it is difficult to see how a reader with no history, biography or psychology could object to the patriarchal assumptions of language. The next chapter looks at what a gendered reader might have to say.

3 Voices

Gendered music

One of the achievements of poststructuralism is a readiness to push beyond standard interpretations and to detect more than one voice in a text. The attraction of such an approach to feminism is clear: if the production and reception of dominant methods of signification are governed by patriarchal interests, then poststructuralism offers much scope for uncovering a submerged feminine voice. Such a voice, however, requires something more substantial than the rhetorical concerns pursued by much poststructuralism, and tends to be rooted in a politics of identity. Feminism, accordingly, tends to move between disembodied patterns of signification and embodied authorial or readerly identity, feeding the perennial debate over whether gender is constructed or intrinsic. This dilemma lies at the heart of gender studies, which developed out of feminism and seeks to understand the constructions of gender that run through a wide range of discourses. It is sympathetic to feminism's aims, but is not restricted to the study of women and femininity. Both fields have contributed to the emergent feminine voice in musicology.

Feminism has been a major component in literary studies for the past thirty years and plays a major role in cultural studies, prompting some of the most exciting work in both these areas. Its influence was slower to find a place in musicology for reasons that feminists have been keen to explain. These relate to general explanations of why musicology has been resistant to critical theory, but also have a more specific dimension. The formalist and positivist reluctance to view music as a form of signification worked to exclude the idea that gendered codes might be ingrained in music and its institutions. In this sense, an aversion to feminism sits alongside an aversion to other approaches, such as reception theory. There is, however, an important difference: the canon that musicology constructs, codifies and studies was until recently virtually entirely male and its institutions were also dominated by men. Methodology oriented to the study of femininity in music is inclined to view this situation of crucial importance, and is therefore more likely to challenge the institutions of musicology than, say, a passing interest in semiotics.

Given the overwhelming gender imbalance in the canon, it was not surprising that the first efforts in feminist musicology followed the lead of literary theory and were directed at the study and documentation of female artists. Such projects dispute unstated priorities, but can use standard procedures to investigate music by women without immediately threatening positivist methodology. Nevertheless, writing about female composers proved to be more of a challenge than the comparable task in literary studies, which already had some writers at its disposal. Virginia Woolf and Jane Austen did not have to be found, even if the distinctive qualities of their writing were still to be explored; but there were few, if any, women composers available for study in the same way: they had to be discovered, and discovered they were. Such finds include the twelfth-century abbess Hildegard of Bingen, the seventeenth-century Italian Barbara Strozzi and figures such as Clara Schumann, who had previously existed only as the wife of Robert Schumann, and Fanny Mendelssohn, who had lived in her brother's shadow. Later composers such as Ethel Smyth and Ruth Crawford Seeger were not unknown, but their music was associated with categories such as English or American music, which tended to deflect gender-oriented study.[1] The recent publication of a biography of Crawford both marks her importance and widens discussion to include the conflicts she endured trying to combine the demands of modernist composition and motherhood.[2]

In order to understand the challenges facing female authors, it is necessary to understand the mechanisms that control the process of canon formation. The patriarchal nature of canon production (and of Freudian psychology) is clearly demonstrated in Harold Bloom's well-known book *The Anxiety of Influence*, which seeks to explain the way poets relate creatively to their ancestors by means of a Freudian, Oedipal theory of sons overpowering their fathers. Poems, states Bloom, are not closed works, they are open and intertextual, communicating with earlier influences. Faced with the achievements and authorial power of established poets, those who would emulate them experience anxiety. The successful poets of the new generation react to that anxiety, he argues, by misreading their predecessors in an attempt to establish their own voices. According to this account, poetic success and a place in the canon is a matter of a resolutely patriarchal power struggle between fathers and sons in which the voice of the father must be subdued. Such an avowedly masculinist theory is not of immediately obvious benefit to feminists, but becomes more useful when understood as a frank analysis of the masculine values embedded in canon construction.[3] To condemn the theory for its masculine discourse is to misconstrue it, since its merit is not that it recommends a patriarchal discourse, but that it analyses the one in which poetry is situated and draws attention to its gendered operation, rather than assuming that such processes are natural and undeserving of comment. As an accurate theory of poetic prestige, it does at least show what women need to overcome.

Where do women poets stand in this battle for cultural supremacy? This is the question asked by Sandra Gilbert and Susan Gubar, who comment that because there is no female equivalent to the Oedipus complex, one cannot simply reverse Bloom's analysis to accommodate female experience. The female writer is likely to experience the tradition as something that offers two female stereotypes (angel or monster), which stifle creativity and lead to an 'anxiety of authorship'. Her struggle, for Gilbert and Gubar, therefore is 'not against her (male) precursor's reading of the world but against his reading of *her*'.[4] And to overcome this impediment she is likely to seek a female precursor as a model, not as a rival to be overpowered. She will be inclined to seek solidarity with a female writer, who has also been marginalized by 'the great tradition', and to look for mutual support rather than struggling for supremacy.

Before pursuing this line of enquiry any further, we need to enquire whether Bloom's theory is of any relevance for understanding lineage and reputation in music. Resemblances are not hard to find. Joseph Straus's *Remaking the Past* uses an explicitly Bloomian model to consider how twentieth-century composers have experienced the anxiety of influence. Discussing Bartók, Stravinsky, Schoenberg, Berg and Webern, he argues that their music is intertextual in the sense that it alludes to earlier music, but references the past in the more general sense of a style that is 'misread' in order to appropriate material for its own purposes. (Boulez's serialist analysis of *The Rite of Spring*, discussed in the previous chapter, illustrates the tendency.) Accordingly, Straus talks of the anxiety of style, noting that Stravinsky speaks of tradition as 'strong pincers', while Schoenberg's belief that his technical innovations would continue the great tradition is well known.[5] Even if composers experience a stylistic Oedipal anxiety that is less acute than the one found in literary rivalry, it still takes place in a male canon and reinforces Bloom's account of masculine primacy.

So how do female composers cope with this state of affairs? Unlike female authors they do not have an established nineteenth-century tradition from which to draw sustenance, but like their literary counterparts they are able to pull creativity away from combative protocols. The tendency for women composers to avoid big public genres such as the symphony and the concerto indicates a desire to work in an arena that is not dominated by a struggle for ascendancy. If we expand our sense of music history beyond the competitive arena of public genres, the history of women in music emerges more clearly. The pioneering study by Jane Bowers and Judith Tick augments music history not only by adding outstanding individuals, but also by considering the history of women in music as a distinct historical group.[6] This strategy enables them to discuss women's roles as musicians in the domestic sphere, as performers and teachers, and to consider their absence from prestigious public genres. And it is not only in the art tradition that female performers have been an unsung presence; they are also abundant in nineteenth- and twentieth-century popular traditions. Indeed, performance is perhaps the area in which women have been most consistently present, particularly as singers, from seventeenth-century Italy to the present day. Because musicology has been so concerned with the authority of text, performance – and women's participation in it – has been neglected.[7] Tending to these neglected areas not only expands history, it also challenges the prevailing norms by disputing the marginalization of women's contributions.

Bloom's masculinist account of canon formation suggests that gender study can be taken further than the documentation of women in music (valuable though it is), to consider investigation of gender constructions in music and its institutions. Not surprisingly, feminism pays a good deal of attention to the aesthetics of autonomy, since (narrowly construed) it is the mechanism that blocks socialized reading of music. Indeed, Suzanne Cusick identifies the doctrine of 'the music itself' as 'the ultimate feminist issue', because the image of autonomy maps onto the cultural norms of masculinity.[8] In order to uncover the gender coding built into the idea of 'the music itself', we need to examine the premisses of music theory. In the previous chapter we saw how theories claiming to offer disinterested, objective descriptions of musical structure founder on their own rhetorical devices. Analysis does not just describe an event, it performatively helps to bring it into being; and it brings into being a view of music that is based on the unity of internal relationships; that prioritizes certain events over others; and that seeks structural coherence rather than social meaning. The rise of instrumental music in the nineteenth century to the highest condition of music – a position upheld by much twentieth-century analysis – marks the ascendance of a music in which the social trace is the most embedded and hardest to track. With no words or obvious social function to give such music meaning, it might indeed seem that, as Hanslick contends, 'the content of music is tonally moving forms'.[9]

Gender theorists argue against such reductions that classical forms – particularly sonata form, which can be reduced to neat structural diagrams – are by no means neutral or value-free: they embody gendered values. A first-movement sonata form, as we saw in the previous chapter, can be seen as a quest narrative: the bourgeois hero is introduced in the familiar surroundings of the home key; meets a less assertive form of subjectivity in the second subject; faces the world in the development (where the now established material is taken to distant territory); and returns to a home environment in the recapitulation (where the second subject is absorbed into the tonic key). And a similar archetypal narrative of progress through life can be attributed to the four-movement sonata. Drawing on the work of narratologists, Susan McClary argues that sonata form's normative model suggests an active male depicted against the backdrop of a female foil, typically a second subject (as theme or key or both) that is subjugated, or assimilated, in the narrative quest and resolution.[10]

As McClary acknowledges, the other that the narrative subdues need not always be the feminine, but she has examined the semiotic codes often used in music theory to describe the second subject, which frequently associate it with a weak, yielding femininity. This trait is representative of a more general tendency to feminize the particular (detail in music), an inclination that undercuts some of the more abstract claims made for instrumental music. In a treatise published in 1845, A.B. Marx described sonata form in explicitly gendered terms, talking of a vigorous and decisive dominant theme and gentler second theme. The latter, he comments, is 'cultivated more flexibly than vigorously – the feminine, as it were, to that preceding masculine. In this sense', he continues, 'each of the two themes is different and only with the other becomes something higher, more perfect.'[11] Thus not only are themes gendered, but the form itself resembles something like an idealized marriage where sexual difference is sublated into a higher union. A more aggressive version of this model was published by Vincent d'Indy in 1909, who having gendered first and second subjects comments: 'It is as if, after the active battle of the development, the being of gentleness and weakness has to submit, whether by violence or persuasion, to the conquest of the being of force and power.'[12] In less overt terms, the cadential metaphor of a 'feminine ending' demonstrates that such semiotic coding also extends to smaller syntactic units, and has survived from the nineteenth century, making an appearance in a dictionary entry of 1970 that talks of a normal masculine cadence ending on a strong beat and a less standard feminine cadence ending on a weak beat.[13] What does all this mean? Are these metaphors simply examples of an outmoded method of understanding music, or do they still exert some influence? Both, probably. Formalist theory would be embarrassed by such language, yet embodies something related to it in its hierarchical metaphors. Analysis may have shed such overtly metaphorical language, but it persists in undervaluing the sort of detail that is historically associated with feminine values.

Nineteenth-century music for the drawing room, particularly piano music, would have been written in the knowledge that it would be performed by women, who were encouraged to play the piano in domestic confines though not to aspire to professional standards. Consequently, the analytical reception of a genre such as the piano nocturne is influenced by circumstances that deem it to be feminine. Jeffrey Kallberg asks the following question: 'What did it mean – culturally, historically, and musically – that the nineteenth-century audience for this genre was understood as primarily female?'[14] Commentaries on Chopin's nocturnes from the 1830s and 1840s, he notes, persistently refer to the feminine qualities of the genre, while their figural language links it to states such as dreaming and longing. One explanation for this association, we have seen, is that women were the primary consumers of piano music in the early nineteenth century, though this situation did not lead to all piano music being regarded as feminine. Other factors that led to the nocturne being considered a feminine genre were the presence of a prominent ('vocal') melody line and abundant detail. Since most nocturnes, and music criticism, were written by men, Kallberg suggests that the genre embodies a male construction of femininity that encourages women to conform to a stereotypical domestic femininity. This conclusion is substantiated by the story of marginalization he unfolds regarding women and the piano nocturne, and is paralleled by an established tradition in painting in which female subjects are constructed by the male gaze. But left at this, it suggests that the policing of gender formation allows no exception. Can we not find another voice in this socialization of genre? Is it not possible that men experiencing the nocturne were not just constructing an idealized, patriarchal femininity, but also exploring another subject position, a feminine voice outside the normative codes of masculinity? It is not easy to provide a definite response to this question because the two strands are intertwined and change meaning in different contexts.

In the twentieth century music theory and modernist aesthetics have sometimes worked together to generate a view of musical material that prizes innovation and technical development above all else. A dominant strand in modernism values a particular type of progressive composition at the expense of more traditional or contextualized styles of music. Mirroring technological progress in a particular way while obscuring its own social construction, this model fails to consider whose voices might be speaking in music and what concerns they might be addressing. Such largely male discourse has become institutionalized in places such as universities as an official modern music, the voice of prestige. Its achievements in inventing new methods of organization and expression are formidable (and offer resources for all composers), but the notion that the music is nothing but structure is forbidding, since it suggests that personal and intersubjective experience are irrelevant for creativity. Such an aesthetic does little for a composer or musicologist who wishes to let her own subjectivity flow through music.

Gendered subjects are, however, by no means absent from the modernist canon. Recently feminist art critics have scrutinized Picasso's aggressive portrayals of women, asking why critics celebrated their technique but ignored their violent subject matter. Nor are deranged and violated women strangers to twentieth-century music: here we have the mad woman (a familiar nineteenth-century figure) of Schoenberg's *Erwartung*, the eponymous prostitute of Berg's

Lulu, and the protagonist of Babbitt's *Philomel* who sings of surviving a sexual ordeal. In a discussion of the latter piece, McClary points to its absent semantic dimension, making the obvious but necessary point that the subject matter can hardly be irrelevant. Unfortunately, the case is not so clear for Babbitt himself, who only talks about the music in terms of its techniques, leaving us to wonder why he chose this text.[15] Whatever the limitations of these authorial intentions, McClary is able to offer a different and convincing reading, suggesting that she hears in the piece a moving account of how Philomel survives the trauma.[16]

By elevating music to an art-form primarily concerned with structural coherence, music theory marginalizes many aspects of music: its timbre and intensity; its affect on the body and its ability to give pleasure. Until recently, discussion of such topics tended to take place outside mainstream musicology, in fora such as the sociological study of popular music, and in discourses deriving from Barthes's later writings on the body, in which music occupies a privileged place (as we shall see later). A good reason for the suppression of such topics in musicology may be that in Western societies music often has feminine and sometimes queer connotations.[17] Many statements by Charles Ives demonstrate a loathing of such associations: in an essay in which he caricatures classical music critics with names such as 'Rollo' and 'Aunty', he even finds canonic figures such as Bach, Beethoven and Brahms over-emasculated. In his words, 'They couldn't exactly help it – life with them was such that they had to live at least part of the time by the ladies' smiles – they had to please the ladies or die.'[18] Fear of the feminine in music is not usually expressed in such a stark manner, but can nevertheless be detected in more mainstream attitudes. It is one reason why the vocabulary of conducting talks of mastering the score and controlling the orchestra.

Cusick gives a stark illustration of how such fears inform musicology's desire to be perceived as a masculine discipline. Her story concerns the founding of the New York Musicological Society in 1930, later to become the American Musicological Society in 1934, an inaugural event from which Ruth Crawford was excluded by a locked door. Many years later, Cusick relates, Charles Seeger confessed to an interviewer that the suppression of Crawford's contribution was a deliberate attempt 'to avoid the incipient criticism that musicology was "woman's work"'.[19] Cusick concludes from this statement that in an attempt to establish musicology as an academic discipline on par with its neighbours, Seeger and the other founding members were anxious that it not be associated with the 'marginal' work performed by women. Reasoning that gender is a constructed set of behaviours expected of potential child-bearers or potential child-begetters, Cusick proceeds to infer that Seeger must have excluded 'Crawford's body from the room whose door metaphorically defined musicology's boundaries not because she was a potential bearer of children, but because her ways of participating in musical culture were associated in his mind with her potential ways of participating in biological reproduction'.[20] By identifying music with perceptions of femininity in this way, Cusick is then able to suggest that it was not just Crawford, but all of the medium's sensuous qualities that were being shut out from the founding meeting of the AMS: in short, Crawford was barred from an event that was decisive in the making of a discipline which sought to control an aestheticized object while resisting its physical allure.

Lawrence Kramer has given careful consideration to the subject of how and why music is perceived as feminine. He argues that the logic of alterity affects both the idea of music (music as cultural trope) and the way music is studied (music as disciplinary object).[21] When music functions as cultural trope – as an ingredient in a cultural continuum – an external aesthetic feminizes music, rendering it both deviant and transcendental. Made transcendent, music buttresses the autonomous subject; but when perceived as deviant, it is the excluded other – at best a tolerated alterity – portraying a lack in a subject dependent on what it expels. The borders of the masculine subject are simultaneously strengthened by this exclusion and undercut by a binary opposition that makes autonomy dependent on elimination.[22] Placing this argument in the context of Ives's invective, we can see how a virile spirituality is articulated through the banishing of effeminate superficiality.

Turning to music as disciplinary object, we find the pattern of alterity is repeated. In a familiar tale, an emphasis on form and unified closure excludes the sensuous and particular; hence representation of music is caught between the supposedly abstract nature of the medium, as an empty sign, and its sonorous specificity. The pattern of exclusion in which music as cultural trope is perceived as feminine is repeated in a disciplinary imperative that seeks to find self-determining structures that marginalize sensuality. In these binaries, the registers that Jacques Lacan dubs the Imaginary (the arena of ego formation, deriving from pre-linguistic infancy) and the Symbolic (the domain occupied with organizing the world) are held apart (instead of intersecting), so that one type of experience cannot touch the other: instead of accessing the Imaginary, the Symbolic rejects it as deviant or mute. As Kramer argues, such binary oppositions and the alterity on which they depend cannot be easily eradicated. Nevertheless, interpreters who come to understand how this othering works will at least be in a position to envisage musical subjectivities more porous to the Imaginary.

The extent to which music as cultural trope permeates bourgeois life is demonstrated by the socialization of music in painting. Music's value as a sign, with all its dilemmas, is for the Victorian bourgeoisie embodied in the piano, representing in the home worldly wealth and domestic fulfilment. As Richard Leppert argues in a study of music as socialized in painting, the piano had a dual role: on the one hand it would often be decorative and would be an object, like a woman, to be gazed at and prized, on the other hand its music would transcend that materiality. As signifiers of social stability, the piano and its domestic surroundings found their way into colonial households, where they participated in a perverse desire to carry on as if in England. Commenting on a pair of watercolours by Sir Charles D'Oyly entitled, respectively, *The Summer Room in the Artist's House at Patna* and *The Winter Room in the Artist's House at Patna*, Leppert comments: 'Translated to India, as in the D'Oyly watercolours, the wifely motherhood and domesticity imprinted on this imagery accrue cultural significance as confirmations of male triumph, not simply over females who have been domesticated, but over an alien culture rendered harmless, hence allowing the introduction of women and their domestic trappings.'[23] In this environment, the piano signifies both social success and a domestic sanctuary, while its music is supposed to transcend sociality, even though music is a somatic discourse that, like female sexuality, might exceed its frame. Paradoxically, then, the piano, like its female exponents, signifies not only social harmony, but also something that might undo that same synthesis. Accordingly, the paintings Leppert discusses range from portraits of pianists as rigid as their pianos, to images associating pianos with sexualized women: women who might not properly belong in the drawing room because they would need to be sexually tamed to play their part in the domestic economy.[24]

These pictures show that the gendering of music as a social site represented in painting cannot be pinned to a firm signifying code; the same is true of music as the sonorous entity withheld from such visual representation. Music for the drawing room may confirm or unpredictably divert in the private sphere the comfortable passivity that is the complement of the vigorous accomplishment celebrated in the public sphere by the symphony. And if domestic music, as the voice of a sanctioned other, may skew its allocated space, it is equally true that public music may have its domestic moments. Nor is the allocation of genres to assigned spaces entirely stable: symphonies can be played in piano duet and songs can be transported to the concert hall, while the piano sonata is a piano symphony in any forum.

Embodied music

Talk of semiotic codes that link music to a marginalized femininity touches on essentialism, a hotly contested area within gender studies and postmodernist debates. Postmodernism's component discourses have done much valuable work in dismantling ideologies that claim to offer a natural viewpoint, showing the way these positions construct a view of normativity. In uncovering the interests that allegedly disinterested beliefs harbour, these procedures offer what might be called an ideology critique. Nevertheless, there is a tendency for this approach to overreach itself, to overestimate the extent of ideology, by declaring itself to be against essentialism per se. This is not a viable stance: to be anti-essentialist, one would, for example, have to deny that human beings share a common need for food and water. Even so, many forms of essentialism are value-loaded, particularly in the ways sex and gender become amalgamated into fixed behavioural patterns. In the passage quoted earlier, Cusick argues that gender is a constructed set of behaviours expected of potential child-bearers or potential child-begetters, thereby acknowledging a physiological distinction between potential child-bearers and potential child-begetters, while arguing that the attribution of gender to them is a social construction. This is a widely held view within gender studies and has powerful consequences. Because gender is socially constructed, it can be reconstructed and contested; hence gender roles are not simply governed by biological fate.

However, for prominent French feminists such as Hélène Cixous and Luce Irigaray, who advocate a form of feminine writing (*écriture féminine*), the female body is an essential part of femininity and an essential part of what is materialized by patriarchal discourse. 'Write your self. Your body must be heard', recommends Cixous, in an essay that both advocates and exemplifies feminine writing.[25] Both these writers have been sharply criticized, firstly, for attempting to universalize women's experiences along European lines, and, secondly, for mythologizing the female body in a manner that is not obviously helpful to a critique of patriarchy because it masks the social mediation of what seems like immediacy. The latter reproach is only partly deflected by a defence of French feminism which argues that the body, too, is a cultural construction,[26] since mythologizing the body tends to disguise this condition.

Rather than becoming too concerned about what might or might not be regarded as essentialist, it might be better to consider the following question, posed in a literary context by Gilbert: 'If the writer is a woman who has been raised a woman – and I daresay only a few biologically anomalous human females have *not* been raised as women – how can her sexual identity be split off from her literary energy?'[27] So since energy, whether literary or musical, can be applied not only to the production of texts, but to their reception as well, and since physiological women are encultured with feminine attributes, a woman engaged in musical activity will bring feminine qualities to it. Hence it makes sense to talk of a female response to music, since a biological woman cannot simply step out of gendered behaviours expected of her. It is true that one can adopt various subject positions when engaging in cultural activity – indeed this is one of the most enhancing possibilities offered by culture: a man can read or listen for a feminine voice in music or literature, and place himself in the position of a woman experiencing a tradition that is perpetuated from a male viewpoint. But however much he may understand the limitations of masculine discourse, a man is not in the position of a woman who experiences the effects of patriarchy through the gender qualities attributed to her. While it is true that patriarchy also places burdens on men, it does not impose the same pattern of exclusion that it extends to women.

Where does the gendered author leave the authorial voice that died in the previous chapter after the attentions of Barthes? The silencing of this voice was once celebrated because it meant that authorial intention could be supplanted by an active reader, free to subvert hallowed tradition. Yet in another way, Barthes's position can be seen as a corollary of a formalist fascination with text. If the text is imbued with immanent meanings, this argument runs, why bother with the author? When that figure is a woman, this attitude might provide an excuse to read from a male perspective and nullify her feminine voice; in effect to undo the work of scholars in reinstating female perspectives. This is not, however, the whole story because textual subjectivities emerge in Barthes's later somatic writings, some of which touch on music.

A famous essay entitled 'The Grain of the Voice' makes a distinction, following Julia Kristeva, between the linguistic and musical grammar of singing and the materiality of language as it interacts with the body – tongue, glottis, teeth and nose. Even though the author is not reinstated in this essay, the authorial body of the performer is very much present. However, this particular instance should not lead to the conclusion that Barthes replaces the author's voice with the performer's body, since he clearly regards the score as more than a technical medium to be warmed up by the performer. In his discussions of Schumann, he reinvents, one might say, the author, not as the source of unified intention, but as a body within the music. In *Kreisleriana*, he hears 'no meaning, nothing that would permit me to reconstruct an intelligible structure to the work. No, what I hear are blows: I hear what beats in the body, what beats the body, or better: I hear this body that beats.'[28] Later, he continues: 'Schumannian beating is panic, but it is also coded (by rhythm and tonality); and it is because the panic of the blows apparently keeps within the limits of a docile language that it is ordinarily not perceived.'[29]

As Kaja Silverman observes, paraphrasing Barthes's *The Pleasure of the Text*, 'the traditional author's "civil status" and "biographical person" exercise a "formidable paternity" over his work, holding it to phallic rectitude and dominant meaning',[30] and it is this figure that is murdered in the death of the author. What remains is the author's body 'as the support for and agency of *écriture*'.[31] This body appears inside the text and, as we have seen, is frequently referred to as a voice or voices since the body Barthes describes is often dispersed into component features. So, to summarize, we have moved from a position in which musical subjectivity is understood to be a combination of tradition and authorial intention, and thus acknowledged only in a general sense, to a structuralist stance where the active subject is virtually excluded from interpretation, and then, finally, to a scenario in which music is coded through its somatic subjectivities. In the latter case, textual/musical meaning emerges from a mix including the shreds of authorial intention, the voices inscribed in the text, and the subject positions of reader/listeners.

With gendered voices reinstated in music, we can now turn attention to what they say. Much pioneering work in feminist literary criticism was undertaken in relation to nineteenth-century literature, notably in Gilbert's and Gubar's *The Madwoman in the Attic*. This study examines how female characters are portrayed in novels, as well as probing more abstract patriarchal procedures. For musicologists seeking to expand on this work an obvious repertoire is provided by opera, a musico-dramatic genre in which stereotypical gender (and ethnic) roles are vividly portrayed. Even in a dramatic idiom, however, one cannot simply map literary criticism onto musicology, because opera study leads straight into long-contested debates on the relationship between music, words and drama. As we have seen, structuralism favours instrumental music for its integration and is therefore likely to devalue the obvious semantic content of opera. When operatic music is valued by this aesthetic, it is admired for its structural coherence, rather than for its interaction with the drama – almost as if it succeeds despite its dramatic context. As a forerunner of structuralist musicology, Alfred Lorenz's systematic attempt to shoehorn Wagner into the symphonic tradition offers a clear instance of this tendency. Recent theory has debunked the notion that music does not signify, and this realization has enabled us to appreciate opera's multidimensionality. One of these dimensions is obviously plot, and analysis of libretto has taken musicology closer to work happening in other fields.

This convergence is not always reciprocal, of course; indeed Catherine Clément's *Opera, or the Undoing of Women* shows scant regard for musicology and by largely restricting her study to readings of libretti annuls the multidimensional quality of opera. It is, nevertheless, a pioneering feminist study of opera and its author (an active participant in French theoretical debates) is able to bring insights that exceed the constraints of a musicology formerly reluctant to question the ethics of drama. Clément tries to work through a dilemma: on the one hand she loves opera, on the other, she finds in a substantial number of its plots patriarchy working in its most insidious form. Her thesis derives from the simple point that many operas, particularly within the tradition of grand opera, climax with the death of a woman. (This is not, of course, true of all operas – and men die too – but it furnishes enough examples to establish a case.)

These women, she contends, are undone by narratives that require their deaths for satisfactory resolution. Musical closure, it is worth adding, also occurs at these dramatic points; and we might compare this denouement with the return to stability in sonata form, accomplished by the assimilation of alien material. Reading libretti away from the music, Clément argues, shows the plots in all their brutal reality without the sexualized mystification endowed by the score. In her words: 'Whenever I read over the words of opera libretti, at a distance from the music that arouses it in the way a sexual member enraptures a body and brings it to life, I am astonished at their brutality, their blinding clarity.'[32]

Speaking of Giacomo Puccini's *Madam Butterfly*, she continues:

> Pinkerton is a young macho whose language is crude: San Antonio, the dirty-talking commissioner, would have behaved in the same way. The female butterfly is impaled, and the opera draws out the metaphor to its most simplistic application: first a man's sexual member, then a dagger in the body. Butterfly dies the death of Japanese woman, for love of an American.[33]

Butterfly's father, we learn, took his own life with a ceremonial dagger; this same weapon makes an appearance at her wedding to the American officer, Pinkerton, and is also the instrument of her own suicide when she understands that Pinkerton will never return to her. Butterfly loses out twice, once as a woman and once as an Oriental, in two interwoven strands that constitute her status as other. Summarized briefly, Pinkerton marries Butterfly, a geisha girl, to amuse himself while in Japan, creating the opportunity for a love duet. She, however, takes the marriage seriously and sonorously waits for him to return and take her to America. When she learns that Pinkerton has no such intention (he returns with his real – American – wife), she maintains her honour through death. Apart from the big numbers mentioned, this plot provides opportunites for the score to embrace oriental signifiers, such as tam tam strokes and augmented intervals. One might read this libretto as an exposure of a tragic Western indifference to another culture, but it feels more like a backdrop for a display, as if Butterfly's death is a form of intoxication.

This is what Clément means when she talks of music arousing the plot in a sexual manner: she seems to hear music simultaneously as a form of ideology, which disguises the patriarchal brutality that takes place in opera, and as a balm for the damage that occurs. In the second sense it is, for her, 'like a great living, membranous surface where the substances for the continuance of life spring back up'.[34] One side of her view distrusts music's alluring qualities, since they cloud the mind and hide the brutality on stage. The other side of her argument posits music as a medium that enables one to survive those same dramatic events. Heard like this, music is both a source of dangerous mystification and refreshing renewal; it both deceives and caresses. Hence Clément's position touches on the somatic qualities of music that much musicology has ignored, but her attention to these alluring powers obscures the formal and semiotic precision music can bring to staged drama. She does, however, have something interesting to say about the embodied music of female voices: that a truth resides in these operatic voices; a truth that sings of oppression, but like the hysteric, will rise again after defeat. She hears this truth in the celebrated mad scene from Gaetano Donizetti's *Lucia di Lammermoor*, where, in her madness, Lucia defies the plot that had tricked her into marrying the wrong brother, whom she murders, and achieves a reconciliation with the absent brother whom she loves.

Picking up on the idea of embodied voices, Carolyn Abbate has modified Clément's depiction of women in opera by arguing that, as sonorous texture, voices can overcome the plots that threaten to crush them. Since Abbate's chief candidate for a sonorous operatic triumph is *The Ring*'s Brünnhilde, in fairness to Clément one should say that her Brünnhilde is a privileged character, shrewder than her associates in the genre, and canny enough to escape the booby-trapped system of kinship that undoes many of her associates in Wagner's drama. Despite a stagey death by fire, she is a listening figure, sensitive to the narratives that unfurl around her, who acquires power and defies her father. Pursuing this theme, Abbate envisages several voice strands in the figure of Brünnhilde: namely, a 'plot-Brünnhilde' and a person she calls 'voice-Brünnhilde', present both as laughter and as sibylline ear. Plot-Brünnhilde executes the actions found in synoptic accounts of *The Ring*, while voice-Brünnhilde emerges in different strains at various points in the drama, most notably in her final immolation monologue. Abbate's account of Brünnhilde's double voice in the immolation is detailed, but we can extract from it that when Brünnhilde sings of union with Siegfried in the final part of the monologue, as she is consumed by flames, the message that she seeks resolution through joining Siegfried in death is bypassed by the intoxication of her voice that brings back so much music associated with her in the drama.[35] It is her voice that concludes the cycle, therefore, above the plot theme of redemption through love.

Brünnhilde is able to speak in a split voice, partly because, in Abbate's opinion, she embodies a mythical feminine energy, and partly because, as Abbate argues more convincingly, she is a listener, or reader. That is, she listens to the narratives of *The Ring* and hears that they vary as they are repeatedly retold; so by reconstructing what she hears, Brünnhilde builds her own story from the inconsistencies in the master narrative. It is in this capacity, listening as a woman, that she attends to Wotan's monologue in Act II of *Die Walküre*, where the god unfolds the plot of *The Ring* and gives a performative demonstration of entanglement in his own narrative strategies. In listening to Wotan's monologue, what she hears are his uncertainties, and she understands that the story of *The Ring* differs on various hearings and tellings: she grasps that it is a construction, moulded by the voices that retell it; and she realizes that its meanings, even its events, are not fixed and can be revoiced.[36] The dilemma Brünnhilde's critical acumen creates for her is how to act on the discrepancies she perceives. Indeed her knowledge eventually contributes to the collapse of her father's symbolic world.

Abbate's idea of locating a listening ear in the text is a good one, and her suggestion that Brünnhilde's interpretive skills affect the narrative of *The Ring* is compelling. The notion that Brünnhilde embodies an unrestrained feminine energy is also appealing, but it runs into the problems of an essentialized femininity that are encountered in French feminism. One aspect of voice-Brünnhilde (the critical listener) does, arguably, succeed in destabilizing patriarchal expectations, but the other part, the intoxicated voice, for all its capacity to soar above the plot, cannot divert its actuality. As a mythical femininity it remains on the margins of the Symbolic Order, with little political impact until it is applied specifically. In short, the problem with Abbate's enthusiasm for this dimension, for all its brilliance, is that it remains on the mythical level of Wagner's drama.

If we follow Adorno's lead and historicize Wagner's music dramas, their mythology maps onto an emergent nineteenth-century industrialism and its bourgeois order. Applying a comparable historical filter, Slavoj Žižek discerns in Fricka 'the jealous high-society lady, in Brünnhilde a rebellious adolescent daughter of a wealthy merchant, and in Hagen a proto-fascist populist'.[37] Following through this reading (and a less specific one would do), Brünnhilde not only defies her father directly, by preserving Siegmund's life, but also reads against the grain of the patriarchal bourgeois order, refusing to be gripped by its narratives. Her persona, then, is akin to a novelist such as Virginia Woolf, who, though she was not at liberty openly to challenge the prevailing order, found ways subtly to subvert and feminize it. Brünnhilde does, however, possess a property that is only metaphorically available to novelists: her voice. It is this that invests her actions with a particularity and envelops listeners in her sound field. But when historicized, her vocal triumph becomes more concrete.

In an essay whose title, 'Opera; or, the Envoicing of Women', is a riposte to Clément's *Opera, or the Undoing of Women*, Abbate further expands her portrayal of women's sonorous victory. Taking Strauss's *Salome* as its focus, the essay considers, amongst other things, the relationship of performer to author, an issue that, though it extends to men and women, is perhaps of particular importance for women, given the tradition of authorial intention. Abbate argues, reasonably, that the mechanism for dispersing this pattern of signification varies from one genre to another and suggests that within this scheme the performing arts enjoy a particularly effective method of dispersal because they place a voice (an actual voice in the case of opera) between author and audience. Consequently, opera does not so much kill off authorial intention as scatter it amongst the performing voices, who occupy various subject positions and enjoy varying importance. Amid these voices, inevitably, will be female voices embodying a relocated authorial presence by frequently holding the stage. Because female voices have been present through nearly the whole history of opera, they represent an established tradition of women assuming the aura of authority.

If women performers can both dissipate and appropriate authorial strength, how do they fare with that other tradition by which passive femininity is instilled: the male gaze? Not surprisingly, the most extensive work on how women are represented as specular objects has been carried out in feminist art history. Typically, the female model, often nude or semi-nude, looks passively out of the picture, and by failing to return the viewer's gaze, she is constructed as a passive object by the male observer. (This stereotype is regularly translated into the cinema, where the camera frequently functions as a male eye, situating women as visual objects in dynamic male plots.) Furthermore, the visual representation of gender cuts across other social divisions, since the models used in nineteenth-century art were mainly working-class women, sometimes prostitutes, whose images were consumed by middle-class men. In this configuration, sexuality is constructed not only by a male viewer, but one from a particular class.

An interesting discussion of the gaze in a public space (a music space) is offered by Griselda Pollock while considering a painting entitled *In the Loge* (1879) by Mary Cassatt (see Plate 1). The picture shows in the foreground a woman dressed in mourning looking through opera glasses across the plane of the picture at an invisible stage. Though she does not return the viewer's gaze, this woman is depicted, unusually, as an active spectator. But, unknown to her, she is herself the subject of another gaze: that of a distant man who, in imitation, watches her through glasses. As Pollock points out, 'the viewer outside the picture is evoked by being as it were the mirror image of the man looking in the picture'.[38] Thus the pun in the picture thematizes the situation of a woman becoming a spectacle in a public place. The dual role in which the foreground woman is both the subject and object of gazes clearly identifies the opera as a scopophilic space. (If the opera house is no longer quite the place to be seen it once was, the economy of image production and consumption has nevertheless intensified since the nineteenth century through the media of film, TV and fashion, all of which make increasing demands on both men and women.)

Returning to the domain of performance, it is clear that the operatic stage is in the domain of the gaze, but it is not obvious that staring in this arena exerts quite the control it commands in other contexts, since we do not just look at singers, we also listen to them. Is there, then, an auditory equivalent to the stare?[39] Probably not. Unlike the eye, the ear is permanently open, a feature that generates mixed consequences, since while we cannot shut out noise produced by others, we can absorb sounds from any location without making our attention obvious. Because we can overhear conversations without the participants knowing we are paying attention, the ear is potentially more duplicitous than the eye, even though listening does not have the ability to unnerve that directional staring possesses. We might conclude that musical performers envelop the ear of the listener with something like an authorial function that does not surrender signification to the auditory gaze. Whatever opera plots may contrive, we hear them through the resonances of their gendered voices, which are not simply creations of the listener.

Plate 1
The Hayden Collection, 1910. Courtesy, Museum of Fine Arts, Boston. Reproduced with permission.

If the embodied voices of women can surmount patriarchal expectations, then the production of gender identity is not as seamless as sometimes suggested. Music, like any other cultural activity, cannot exist completely outside of the gender norms of its time, but it can offer an arena in which to explore other subjectivities. And it is this possibility that has made Franz Schubert, and the various subject positions to be found in his music, the object of critical attention. In a discussion of 'Die Forelle' ('The Trout'), Kramer analyses the triangular relationship between the narrator, the fisherman and the trout in the context of early nineteenth-century mermaid fancies, which depict women as objects of desire, while also expressing a feminine empathy.[40] The song, in three stanzas, depicts, firstly, a trout swimming in clear waters, secondly, a fisherman on the bank watching the trout, and, thirdly, its capture by the fisherman who muddies the waters. These events are accompanied in the piano by the famous 'leaping figure' (see Ex. 2a), which is 'muddied' in the interlude depicting the capture of the trout (see Ex. 2b).

Kramer gives a number of readings of the song and the set of variations on it found in the *Trout Quintet*, from which two positions for the narrator in the triangular relationship emerge as particularly

Ex. 2a

Ex. 2b

significant. Firstly, the narrator identifies with the trout (a wish to be woman) and hence identifies with the object of the fisherman's desire. This reading is supported by the vocal line's affinities with the leaping accompaniment. Secondly, the narrator is a rival with the fisherman (and forms a bond with him through desire for the same object), hence his blood boils when he sees the fish twisting on the fisherman's rod. With the capture of the fish, he is not only outdone by a more virile man but also loses the shared object of desire. More possibilities are introduced when the song is sung, as it often is, by a woman; a position that is likely to weaken the narrator's rivalry with the fisherman and to increase associations with the fish. It is hard to fix one dominant interpretation on the song, a fact that is itself indicative of music's ability to outmanoeuvre rigid social codes.

Feminism, whether musicological or general, does not provide a uniform analysis of the social construction of gender, and one would be surprised if the situation were otherwise. This is partly because the dominant influences of psychoanalytic and historical approaches are not easily reconciled, and the awkward issue of essentialism lies across their intersection. Nevertheless, widely held conceptions are shared by feminism, and they can be addressed in a musicological context by modifying, as follows, a statement written by Robyn Warhol and Diane Herndl.[41] It is generally agreed that the oppression and marginalization of women is embedded in music, its discourses and institutions. By studying how these attitudes are constructed, we can reorient the reception histories on which such traditions are built and by doing so contribute to a reconstruction of gender, thereby widening the scope of both musicology and feminism. A loose definition, maybe, but it demonstrates that understanding how gender is coded in music illuminates processes that were only dimly sensed before, indicating, for example, why some music elicits specific responses.

Having gendered the formalist abstraction that music was once considered to be, it is as well to consider the accomplishment. What, we might ask, do we do with a canon that is now tarnished by the voice of patriarchy? A good starting place is to recognize that understanding how gender is coded in music will change our perception of the canon, but is not itself a reason to dismiss the latter as ideological baggage. We do not have to be puppets of a particular reception history because we can revoice music to articulate our own concerns. If we examine a work at the heart of the canon, let us say Beethoven's Fifth Symphony, it is hard (indeed perverse) to deny it embodies struggle; and reasonable to hear it as a narrative in which a heroic subject overcomes obstacles and achieves a degree of reconciliation that is not possible in life. But the music is not emptied by that interpretation. The tutti orchestration of the Finale may bathe the listener in a sea of sound that is experienced more as abandon than triumphalism, while the return of the Scherzo in the Finale can be experienced as a moment of doubt in the midst of victory.[42]

Feminism's achievements are substantial, but when harnessed to a populist postmodernism its insights are inclined to merge with generalized attempts to portray Western rationality as a uniform field of oppression, geared primarily to suppression of the particular. This outlook judges the canon harshly and does not facilitate the kind of readings given above of Schubert or Beethoven. While one can see how this position is reached, by rejecting a dysfunctional rationality it fails to see that the same tradition also contains within itself the tools for its own critique. To analyse institutions and show how they marginalize women is a task that requires refined procedures that are principally located in the call to equality found in the tradition they critique. To transform a dysfunctional rationality is to be indebted to an Enlightenment tradition of equality and rigour, even if the equality of women was not originally on this agenda. Furthermore, one cannot occupy a space outside the socio-symbolic order, since a refusal of all social relations is impossible.[43]

One of the most salient characteristics of modernity is its reflexive ability to scrutinize its own assumptions and to modify its own organization. Gender theory is not subsumed by modernity, but it nevertheless taps into this self-reflexive quality and changes modernity in the process. Its insights remain crucial as increasing standardization and homogeneity determine that both sexes are likely to suffer the ornamentalizing effects of a scopic economy. With everyone increasingly observed and assessed, much can be learned from the ways in which women have in the past articulated spaces within the confines of a patriarchal order. Hence aesthetic experience – manifest both in artistic production and its continuation in theory – is important for its ability to, in Kristeva's words, 'break the code, to shatter language, to find a specific discourse closer to the body and emotions, to the unnameable repressed by the social contract'.[44]

Lacanian psychoanalysis

Psychoanalysis is the obvious place to turn to for a discourse of the emotions, and is not surprisingly one of Kristeva's principal interests. Yet psychoanalysis is often written from a male perspective, as we saw in discussing Bloom's Oedipal theory of poetic prestige. Feminism has worked hard to challenge these assumptions, not just in Freud, but in the readings of him that constitute Lacanian psychoanalysis: a body of work that offers significant resources for both gender theory and musicology. We have already seen its vocabulary employed in Kramer's analysis of the splitting of the Imaginary and the Symbolic in discourses designed to buttress music against feminine associations. The logic of binary exclusion Kramer pursues indicates that a blend of psychoanalysis and gender theory provides powerful resources for understanding how music is gendered, how it is valued, and how the voices it embodies can be read and, if necessary, reconstructed.

Gender studies draw mainly on a form of post-Lacanian psychoanalysis that has sought to overcome the patriarchal dogma of its principal influence. As Jacques Lacan enjoys an unrivalled reputation for obtuseness, it is not my intention to provide a summary of all aspects of his thought; nevertheless some concepts do need to be broached. He views the mind as an unstable constellation of three orders: the Imaginary, the Symbolic and the Real. The Imaginary can be understood as a pre-symbolic stage in which the baby is coterminous with the rest of the world. Through association with, and imitation of, the mother's voice, the infant experiences plenitude and a continuity between body and environment. This state is broken by the entry into language, which is associated with the father, and marks the Symbolic Order. (This order is sometimes called 'phallic', particularly by feminists who use the term to highlight the meaning attributed to the phallus by Lacan, as both a symbolized body part and a privileged signifier that offers the prospect of stable meaning.) The Symbolic Order separates the child from an imagined unity, so that the desire for unity with the mother becomes repressed, thereby opening the unconscious. Entry to the symbolic world shatters a certain bliss, but at the same time the child becomes a subject through intersubjective interaction and is consequently able both to structure and be structured by the world. The third component in Lacan's triad, the Real, designates the world and mind as we would experience it without language, personal history or cultural representation. To dwell in the Real is to be psychotic, and we encounter this register as trauma when it leaks into the Symbolic Order.

So what significance do these registers have for music? If we understand the intersections of the Imaginary and the Symbolic as producing a set of differences between sensory, or immediate, and constructed perceptions of the world, then their relevance becomes more obvious. Traditional music theory has much to say about music as a symbolic construct, but little to say about the sense of plenitude it can induce. It represses the sensory side, even though music offers a form of sensuality that is not easily contained by formalist schemes, and in doing so pulls music towards the linguistic Symbolic Order. Music (likewise musicology) cannot, of course, be a domicile of one order to the exclusion of the other: it inhabits both domains, even though one may be more evident in a particular score or performance. The point is that because musicology has, typically, described music as a symbolic object, it has done little to advance understanding of music as an imaginary object.

Addressing this concern, David Schwarz suggests that an instrumental doubling of a vocal line is a particular device for creating an imaginary, or fantasy, object, and relates this mechanism to a stage in infancy where the baby hears a vocal mirror in its mother's voice. By listening to and imitating its mother's voice, the child experiences a sense of abundance, and it is a recollection of this imaginary fulfilment that the voice mirroring of an instrumental vocal doubling attempts to capture. This argument is at once revealing and generalized, like much psychoanalytic discussion of culture. The interest lies in the cultural specificity of how this doubling takes place, and how the imagined space is represented. Schwarz offers two examples: The Beatles' 'I Want You (She's So Heavy)' from the album *Abbey Road* and Schubert's song 'Ihr Bild' ('Her Portrait') from the collection *Schwanengesang* (*Swan Song*). In two verses of 'I Want You' John Lennon sings with a unison blues/rock scat accompaniment on guitar, imitating the instrument with small nuances to indicate the 'grain of the voices' differences'.[45] This effect, Schwarz claims, offers an illusion of the fulfilment of desire that the song describes, 'a fantasy of the acoustic mirror as a fantasy thing',[46] before the intervention of white noise with which it closes. Heine's 'Ihr Bild', meanwhile, portrays the narrator standing before a picture of a lost beloved, whose face seems to come to life as he gazes. The song in ABA form opens with the piano doubling the vocal line, tracking the desired image. This mirror becomes clouded as the image appears to weep (bars 18–22), and the return (bar 24) of the opening music (with small modifications) serves to split the narrator's fusion of memory and desire as the present situation, marked by loss, intrudes.[47]

These songs, with their overt desire and disillusionment, provide quite close analogies to the maternal theme in Lacan's notion of the Imaginary, one within the conventions of rock, the other through the semiotics of nineteenth-century lied. Yet manifestations of the Imaginary need not be closely linked to this model. Kristeva modifies the Lacanian Imaginary to include what she characterizes as an underlying rhythm. She describes this *chora* as pulsions, or quantities of energy that move through the not yet constituted body, which underlie symbolic figurations.[48] Toril Moi describes what happens when the *chora* comes into contact with the Symbolic:

> Once the subject has passed into the Symbolic Order, the *chora* will be more or less successfully repressed and can be perceived only as pulsional *pressure* on symbolic language: as contradictions, meaninglessness, disruption, silences and absences in the symbolic language . . . It constitutes, in other words, the heterogeneous, disruptive dimension of language, that which can never be caught up in the closure of traditional linguistic theory.[49]

Kristeva envisages a somatic linguistic practice open to the work of the *chora* in the construction of signification, and hopes that such an application might destabilize the phallocentric Symbolic Order. Because a pulsional energy is less repressed in music than elsewhere in the Symbolic Order, it outlines indistinctly the symbolic practice that Kristeva envisages. Indeed Kristeva is invoked by Barthes in 'The Grain of the Voice' when he listens for the material of signification in the singing voice. Consequently, musicology as a medium for reading such pulsions is well placed to augur a less regimented Symbolic Order. But we should remember that it can only modify the Symbolic Order, not abandon it. Furthermore, the *chora*'s disruptive effect on language is not inherently a good thing, since pulsional energy is undirected and susceptible to ideology. Its ability to unsettle fixed meaning is only creative if it functions within the Symbolic Order to enable enriched intersubjective communication.

Even as conveyed by Lacan, the Symbolic Order is not a realm of fixed signification. It is also the domain of the unconscious, that which he calls the discourse of the other. This othering is within the order itself, since it describes the systems that individuals both determine and are determined by in the process of creating meaning and interpreting the world. The unconscious, then, is already at work in signification as a sort of second reading, a second voice within the sign system. Music is encountered as the discourse of the other when we experience ourselves being addressed by it: that is, when we feel personal memories are being organized and relocated by something outside of ourselves, inserting us in a domain of intersubjectivity. Musical experience is shot through with a desire for reconciliation, but is also continually frustrated because, as Lacan comments (in an insight anticipated by the philosopher Arthur Schopenhauer), desire is constantly deferred by its own desire for itself. Put another way, what desire desires is desire. The consequences of this splitting within signification are far-reaching, as the poststructuralist fascination with elusive origins demonstrates. It is a manifestation of the idea we encounter with Derrida that one cannot step outside a text and impose fixed meaning on it. Looked at like this, we can see that the mirage of authentic performance, which exerts a grip across a broad spectrum of music (including classical and popular), is a search for an imaginary object unaffected by the othering within consciousness. This musical imago does not, of course, exist, but a deluded pursuit of it may, nevertheless, produce fine results.

As mentioned, the Lacanian mental map is a triad comprising the Imaginary, the Symbolic and the Real. So far, we have looked at two components of this triad, but not the third, the Real. This does play a role in music, but is not often heard. Its auditory manifestation would be a world without symbolic intervention, that is to say, just unprocessed noise – a collapse of social relations that would be described as psychotic. Since the Real, because of what it is, is not easily understood, it is helpful to turn again to visual art for a model. One area in which we experience the Real is trauma – a mental experience that is not entirely assimilated into the Symbolic. In a chapter entitled 'The Return of the Real' (like the whole book) Hal Foster discusses pictures by Andy Warhol, such as *Ambulance Disaster*, that stage the Real as trauma, in this particular case by showing a crashed ambulance, with a corpse hanging out of the window. But the Real is not trauma as such, even if encountering it is invariably a traumatic experience. It receives perhaps its most compelling and disturbing projection in a series of images produced by Cindy Sherman in the 1980s, concentrated around the theme of a pulsatile mass. *Untitled #190* is a conglomerate of slimy matter, suggesting a mixture of food remains and bodily excretions, possibly even the inside of the body, from which protrudes an obscene face; what Foster calls an 'evil eye with a visage of its own'.[50] The pulsatile mass is probably as close as we can approximate to a representation of the Real. Moreover, the eye protruding from it – a symbolic construct – makes it gaze at us, as if we are situated by the Real, and ensures that the whole thing is perceived as disgusting.

Perhaps the auditory equivalent of this might be to hear noise at an unpleasant level that blocks social functioning and makes us feel trapped in something alien. Schwarz gives several examples of the Real, one in the The Beatles' 'I Want you (She's so Heavy)' discussed earlier. The song moves to its final phase with a yell from Lennon that precipitates a seemingly endless (trapped) repetition of the chorus, heard against a wall of white noise, as a sort of wind effect, that becomes louder, eventually matching the volume of the guitars. This event signifies the Symbolic Order of musical coherence collapsing into the Real.

Obviously, the Real is not an area in which music, or any other cultural form, can dwell for long since it breaks down the symbolic contract that constitutes culture. However, the recent fascination with the Real, which manifests itself both in theory (especially of popular culture)[51] and visual arts does signify a shift in perspective away from art as text to something we may tentatively call identity. As Foster comments, experience represented as trauma simultaneously asserts and erases the subject: the subject is there in the sense that trauma cannot be dispersed in signification, but at the same time it is an empty subject that is portrayed. He writes: 'in this way trauma discourse magically resolves two contradictory imperatives in culture today: deconstructive analyses and identity politics. This strange rebirth of the author,' he continues, 'this paradoxical condition of absentee authority, is a significant turn in contemporary art, criticism, and cultural politics.'[52] Crucially, identity politics curb the universalizing tendencies of psychoanalysis, confronting them with historically embedded discourses. Without identity politics, the discussion of popular music that follows would be impossible.

4 Identities

Theoretically informed musicology understands both art and popular musics as social constructions. Nevertheless, the study of popular music raises specific issues, the most obvious being the absence of a musicological tradition to build on. Mainstream musicology has, until recently, largely ignored popular music because an overtly socialized medium appeared trivial alongside music making claims to autonomy. Conversely, the social immersion of the same medium is what makes it obviously attractive for sociologists and, more recently, cultural theorists. Since technique and social identity are interlinked, the only sensible way for popular music studies to proceed is on the basis of an interdisciplinary awareness willing to traverse various methodologies, all vying to shape the disciplinary object in a particular way.[1] The ingredients of this mix will vary according to research aims: a project that involves observations on youth culture, for example, is likely to have a strongly sociological dimension. Problems only arise when any contributory discipline tries to obviate the claims of others. Now that art music is also studied as a contextual medium, musicology is becoming increasingly familiar with strategies accepted in the study of popular music. This shared concern may well dissolve the high/low divide, since it prefers to understand what music does in a particular tradition than to measure it against pre-established criteria. Before expanding on the prospects of a context-sensitive musicology, however, it is worth examining the various approaches that have characterized popular music studies.

In the space of a single chapter these are necessarily selective, but have been chosen to amplify themes such as essentialism and gender that occur elsewhere in the book, and to show how musical subjectivities are constructed. The first section examines attempts to understand the production processes of popular music, and looks at how culture is socially embedded. It also considers the competing claims made by sociological and musicological readings, with a view to better interdisciplinary understanding. The second part turns to value and authenticity, considering how music can reflect on its component discourses and explaining why some performance styles and traditions are considered to be more authentic than others. The third section considers how identity is constructed in music and contemplates what it means for music to offer a range of subject positions to be readily exchanged and consumed.

Critique

In Chapter 1 we encountered Adorno as an early exponent of critical musicology, exploring the social antagonisms of modernism, while clinging to the utopian aspirations of bourgeois art. But this was not the only arena in which he worked: the other face of modernism for him is the culture industry with its promise of fulfilment through mass-produced entertainment. In developed capitalist societies he finds a widespread acceptance of a standardized culture that, in his opinion, exerts an authoritarian grip on popular consciousness. This view is embodied in the culture industry chapter of *Dialectic of Enlightenment* (a volume co-authored with Max Horkheimer), which considers the industrialized production of culture in a discussion ranging over television, film and music. Fredric Jameson remarks that 'the Culture Industry is not a theory of culture but the theory of an *industry*, of a branch of the interlocking monopolies of late capitalism that makes money out of what used to be called culture'.[2] This comment is extreme but nonetheless helpful, since Adorno's topic is indeed the commercialization of life and the conditions in which culture is produced. He describes a closed system in which the production of predigested culture determines reception, in which, as he puts it, 'the composition listens for the listener'.[3]

His view of consumer culture consolidated in the 1930s and 1940s (he lived in the United States from 1938 to 1949), and was based on encounters with B movies, jazz-influenced dance music and a conformist era of Tin Pan Alley.[4] As examples, he provides stereotypical film situations where one knows who will be punished and rewarded: the hero and the spoilt heiress he defies are both characters who, in Adorno's words, 'never do anything more than fulfil the purpose allotted them in the overall plan'.[5] His reading, in this vein, of a film cliché in which the female typist, who just happens to conform to the current fashion in beauty, hopes for fulfilment through the attentions of her male boss also says much about the gender conditioning of what he calls the overall plan. Such situations form part of the seamless continuum in which the administered world operates. The entertainment offered outside working hours, according to this scheme, is subject to the same mechanisms experienced in the workplace, perpetually defer-ring dreams of fulfilment.

With its unwavering theme of ideological deception, Adorno's theory of the culture industry is an unlikely place to look for a methodology appreciative of popular music. But, as ever with Adorno, the picture is complex. His sociology of music is significant for bothering to study popular culture at all; for analysing the impact of industrialized cultural production; and, crucially, for placing art and popular musics within the same arena of modernization. In a famous letter to his friend Walter Benjamin, Adorno comments that mass art and high art are 'torn halves of an integral freedom, to which however they do not add up'.[6] The import of this statement is that each half plays the other to its partner: while the one assumes critical responsibility, the other offers enjoyment, consequently the two halves are pushed apart. Significantly, this division is not along lines of social transcendence and social immersion, since both musics exist in a socialized continuum. This vital point is often missed when Adorno's culture industry essays are portrayed as unremittingly elitist and negative.

Nevertheless, the limitations of Adorno's understanding of popular music need to be acknowledged. He writes as if all popular songs follow a single formula designed to generate passive consumption. In support of this view, he cites Abner Silver's and Robert Bruce's textbook, *How to Write and Sell a Hit Song* (1939), which does indeed provide a basic frame for composing custom-built songs.[7] Working on this basis, Adorno proposes that popular song values an 'originality' sufficient only to register a difference from the regular model without unsettling expectations. Such 'originality', accordingly, is a sign of 'pseudo-individualization';[8] a pretence of individuality catered for by the system and serving to endorse standardization.

A similar critique is levelled at jazz, in which he finds a message of spontaneity and freedom stamped by conformity.[9] Adorno's views on jazz fuel the controversial nature of his work on the culture-industry theory because a medium that for many offers an alternative to dominant cultural values is held by him to be the embodiment of just such a currency. His opinions compel us to ask what Adorno understood by jazz. It seems that he chose to take the jazz-influenced dance music of Paul Whiteman's band as typical, even though it is likely that he at least knew of the 'Hot Jazz' associated with figures such as Sidney Bechet and Louis Armstrong. The problem is that he makes little distinction between the two styles and uses Whiteman to condemn all jazz; a position that strengthens the clout of the culture-industry theory, but does scant justice to the field of jazz.[10]

It appears, then, that Adorno's perception of popular culture was already selective in the 1930s, and it became increasingly so as the years passed and his opinions remained unchanged. By understanding popular music as a degraded form of the bourgeois tradition, he failed to appreciate the diversity of its repertoire and misrepresented the specific social circumstances of much musical production. Insensitive to the particulars of class and ethnicity, he was reluctant to concede that American popular music derives from various traditions and communities that are not simply homogenized into a single culture. He ignored the African roots in jazz and the Blues, and was apparently unaware of the mechanisms by which European folk traditions were preserved by immigrant communities in America.[11] In his defence, however, it is worth noting that an excessive emphasis on the specifics of social groups and their musics misses the ways in which identities are mediated by the social totality.

A symptom of Adorno's generalized approach is that he often misses strategies of resistance in popular musics that strive to offer something other than homogeneity, even though his own ideas are helpful in locating such moments. Indeed, Richard Middleton describes the Blues in terms redolent of Adorno's modernist aesthetics as 'the expression of alienated subjectivity caught within oppressive social structures',[12] and many find a similar impulse in rock. Moreover, Adorno's work (mainly on art music) on how established musical procedures are contested offers some guidleines for how popular culture might repel a seamless cycle of production and reception. His Mahler monograph provides a good starting place for such a search, since it discusses Mahler's ability to derive new meanings from familiar procedures. Drawing on Adorno's idea that Mahler creates a second life for worn material, Max Paddison seeks a similar critical impulse in rock music, finding that Frank Zappa's albums reflect on their own commodity status.[13] When, however, one considers the marked overlaps between the discourses of new music and those of experimental rock, it is not surprising that such parallels can be drawn. Despite Zappa's achievement, therefore, we must clearly look further afield than material innovation to locate value in popular music that does not aspire to the condition of new music. Without rejecting the idea of socialized material, musical understanding needs also to include a range of textual and contextual procedures. A critical trace in popular music might, for example, be found in recording method, vocal quality, intertextual reference or choice of venue.

The prospect of just such new interpretive practices informs Walter Benjamin's optimistic assessment of the democratizing potential of new technology, which sparked lively exchanges with Adorno. Benjamin's most famous essay on the subject, 'The Work of Art in the Age of Mechanical Reproduction', chooses film as its medium, but has much to say that is of relevance to music technology. Caught between nostalgia and belief in the new, Benjamin discusses what he calls aura in traditional art (an idea closely linked to autonomy), which he describes as an object's ability to appear distant however close it is to the viewer. The reproductive technology of photography erodes aura, according to Benjamin, because something that can be copied cannot be unique. When aura wears down, so do the moorings that tie art to tradition and authority; consequently meaning becomes more dependent on how an object is situated by viewers. In this way, Benjamin anticipates more active cultural participation than Adorno, but fails to theorize how film technology, especially, is mediated by the culture industry. Nevertheless, even if his optimism loses ground to Adorno's more searching analysis of cultural production, Benjamin proffers a cultural practice whose significance lies in what Middleton calls its 'positioning within the process of production'.[14] This is to say that the ways in which we understand the technologies of art and situate ourselves within them are an intrinsic part of cultural meaning.

So far, we have examined theories of popular culture from within the tradition of Frankfurt critical theory; to pursue the significance of location further, we need to turn to cultural studies, an intrinsically interdisciplinary field, crossing through literary criticism, history and sociology. Early texts include E.P. Thompson's *The Making of the English Working Class* and Raymond Williams's *Culture and Society*. In a later essay, 'The Future of Cultural Studies', Williams explains that, because an intellectual or artistic project cannot be understood aside from its formation (loosely understood as social context), the goal of cultural studies is to understand both project and formation. It aims not merely to see one in terms of the other, but to understand both as different ways of materializing what he calls 'a common disposition of energy and direction'.[15] The upshot for music is that it matters who is singing a song and how it is disseminated, and it also matters how the sounds are assembled, but the two are not merely related: they are interdependent. Therefore, it is not surprising that Williams's understanding of culture extends beyond acknowledged cultural artefacts to communicative traditions, what he calls 'structures of feeling'. Since, to paraphrase one of his essay titles, culture is ordinary, newspaper articles and television programmes demand his attention as well as canonic texts.

Such everyday culture became a preoccupation of the Birmingham-based Centre for Contemporary Cultural Studies. Like Adorno's sociology of music, the work produced at this centre is dependent on the notion of ideology, but examines patterns of resistance, rather than assuming that consumption is passive. It investigates youth cultures, including their codes of dress and musical styles, as practices that scorn the standards expected of them. A well-known text to have emerged from this tradition is Dick Hebdige's *Subculture: The Meaning of Style*. In the chapter on punk Hebdige gives inventories of style, which include ornamental safety pins, spiky, dyed hair, shredded clothes, robotic dancing and raucous music. In punk, he concludes, working-class youth showed its disdain for accepted behaviour by semiotically recoding a range of commodities and accepted values. This is a subculture that is impossible to understand purely, or even partly, in musical terms, since much of it negates musical values. A virtue is made of scanty technique and the resulting abrasive sound. Johnny Rotten puts the matter more succinctly when he comments: 'we're into chaos not music'.[16]

Cultural studies' willingness to move away from text-based methodologies is clearly an essential requisite for understanding such a social formation. As Richard Johnson puts it, 'the ultimate object of cultural studies is not, in my view, the text, but *the social life of subjective forms at each moment of their circulation*, including their textual embodiments'.[17] One is, however, bound to point out that subjective forms achieve stronger configurations in some texts than others. Musicology has much to gain from understanding music as a social energy, but is understandably reluctant completely to abandon textualized notions of music. And it is significant that while the definitions of cultural studies given by Williams and Johnson do not place the text at the centre of the inquires, neither do they destroy it. This stance contrasts with much discussion of popular music that has nothing to say about how it sounds. Such writing is not inherently vacuous, but it does omit a significant dimension. The challenge is to consider the specificity of the sounds and their social formation simultaneously.

Studying popular music requires musicology to expand not just its view of acceptable repertoires but its notions of acceptable methodologies. It is surprising, then, that recent analytical work on rock music should shun contextual study in favour of technical discussion. John Covach, for instance, accepts that popular music articulates social meanings, but is not especially interested in them: 'the problem', he writes, 'lies in the assertion that there is a single way to view popular music: namely, as inherently and primarily social'. Covach's suggested corrective primarily takes the form of an inversion: 'that popular music can also be considered as inherently *musical*, and only secondarily social'.[18]

Yet although one can see how he reaches this position, surely the point is that the social and the musical are not easily separated like sheep and goats because sounds always occur in specific social contexts.[19] Granted, some genres of popular music can be successfully addressed in technical terms (most of the Beatles' songs fall into this category), a dimension that has been neglected for too long. Nevertheless, the material remains socially mediated, not least by dint of its own popularity. Formal analysis is not, furthermore, applicable to all popular musics, and part of Covach's limitation is that he seems to assume work within a particularly narrow definition of the genre, namely rock, while making generalized assumptions. Surely to look for prolongations or interesting melodic construction in, say, punk or rap is to look for features that are not valued in these genres.[20] This is not to suggest that one music is social and another musical: all music is social, but in some cases musical processes can be discussed without reference to the social forms they embody, while elsewhere cultural and musical organization cannot be (even temporarily) separated.

Covach's argument is rooted in music theory and is as much about this discipline as it is about popular music, since he is fearful of his community being overcome by a sociological methodology. Broadening music theory to include what is generally called 'theory' in other humanities subjects need not be so threatening because it would facilitate dialogue with other disciplines, and confirm the emerging consensus that popular music cannot be understood without recourse to wide-ranging methodologies.[21] Such a blend would be able to link technical comprehension to the specific social contexts in which sounds are organized. Adorno's culture industry theory did at least envisage such an amalgam, even if its focus on interlocking monopolies turned attention away from the detailed social life of particular musical practices.

Value

The social configurations that organized sounds become associated with, and create, tend to attribute value to music. Of course, the meanings of sounds change as the mix of social and musical codes varies, but when special value is attached to a particular combination, subsequent modifications may be found wanting in comparison with the 'authentic' version. The idea of authenticity has extensive ramifications in the codification of music. In Chapter 2 we saw how it is routed through the concept of fundamental structure and is also key to the practice of historically informed performance. Implicit in such approaches is the belief that origin and copy can be separated, a view that Derrida has done much to undermine. However, the subsequent discussion of gender studies in Chapter 3 demonstrated that deconstructing voice and presence leads to mixed results. This is because destabilizing rigid orthodoxies may be productive, but shaking valued identities will not always be appreciated. This tension, not surprisingly, is apparent in popular music, where one needs to tread a fine line between scrutinizing rigid beliefs and upsetting particular values. The problem is that value becomes harder to quantify when it no longer rests on a bedrock of authenticity. We need, therefore, to examine the mechanisms for constructing authenticity before considering how value might be reconstructed.

Studies of English folk song are shot through with contested notions of authenticity. Cecil Sharpe's *English Folk Song: Some Conclusions* (published 1907) is built around an idealized bourgeois vision of rural communities. These communities, he argues, are uncontaminated by modernity and preserve a body of folk song that springs from a musical intelligence expressive of the nation. Sharpe's peasant singers are uneducated and ignorant of art music, yet they are also noble and through natural ability preserve a music that stems anonymously from the past. Such imagery paints an ideology of nation in which rural values are pitted against urban industrialism. Writing sixty years later, A.L. Lloyd provides a modified version of this outlook when he turns his attention to the working-class music ignored in Sharpe's arcadian dream, taking a particular interest in the songs of weavers and miners.[22] In doing so, he expands the sphere of folk song and modifies Sharpe's boundaries, but does not eradicate them.[23] Lloyd distinguishes between authentic song, which arises from within the community, and popular song, written for performance in music halls, pubs and clubs; in the process he transfers Sharpe's ideology from the peasantry to the working class. For Sharpe and Lloyd, then, authentic folk song is something that arises directly from a particular experience, while holding at bay new forms of social organization, particularly those deriving from urban life. This distinction allows them to construct a category of folk music that is separate from bourgeois art music and from commercial popular music. Such partitions are, of course, increasingly difficult to sustain since borders are frequently crossed.

The imaginary landscape of English folk-song scholarship is recognizable in Bartók's views on Hungarian peasant music, though recast in a spiky, modernist context. He makes a passionate distinction between the gypsy café music that influenced the Hungarian music of Liszt and the Polish music of Chopin, and the ancient peasant music heard in remote villages, untouched by modern living. Gypsy music, in his intolerant opinion, is blemished by hackneyed patterns from popular music and romantic sentimentality. Peasant music, by contrast, shows a markedly different range of characteristics:

> The right type of peasant music is most varied and perfect in all its forms. Its expressive prose is amazing, and at the same time it is devoid of all sentimentality and superfluous ornaments. It is simple, sometimes primitive, but never silly. It is the ideal starting point for a musical renaissance, and a composer in search of new ways cannot be led by a better master.[24]

In a strange combination of nationalism and modernist experimentation, Bartók finds in Hungarian peasant music an antidote to romantic excess, and locates a resource for musical revival. He hears this music in a particular way, focusing on its technical features (rather than its social functions) and feeds this premodern medium into modernist construction. Stravinsky also took inspiration from indigenous folk song but, less idealistic than Bartók, found occasion to deny such authenticity in the cosmopolitan environment of Paris.[25] These visions are underpinned by a shared belief (notwithstanding Stravinsky's duplicity) that a jaded modernity can be revived by the crystal waters of national identity.

Based on the idea of inside values polluted by outside sources, this pattern remains influential. It is found, for example, in the controversy over Bob Dylan going electric. When Dylan played acoustic guitar and harmonica he was valued by a folk community that felt rejected when he transferred to electric guitar and used rock-style amplification. This story reveals the folk audience to be unprogressive, but it also shows that the emergent rock community was developing its own conventions. Thus the divide that Dylan crossed is not as wide as either the folk or rock aficionados might have supposed, since rock takes from folk the notion of a musical community based on shared values. By doing so, rock transfers the ideology of folk to a music that, in Simon Frith's words, is 'without doubt, a mass-produced, mass-consumed, commodity'.[26] This brand of authenticity is then invoked to distinguish rock from pop, to suggest that the former articulates genuine, shared experience, while the latter produces the sort of standardized products that Adorno describes (and which are often considered to be feminine). However, since both rock and pop are mass-produced commodities, to pretend that rock eludes this condition is clearly an illusion.

Frith shows how Bruce Springsteen depends on a manufactured and marketed authenticity. Focusing on *Bruce Springsteen and the E Street Band Live* of 1986, he argues that the vast commercial success of this live set became what he calls 'that ultimate object of capitalist fantasy',[27] a product whose commercial success itself generated further sales: that is to say, an object whose prosperity derives from the commercial process it instigated, rather than from its intrinsic worth. Yet, despite this state of affairs, Springsteen, ironically, is marketed as quite the reverse, as the real thing: despite his immense wealth, he wears worker's clothing, works hard on stage and visibly sweats. This brand of reality manifests itself in an identification with the working class through familiar themes of poverty, love and hope. But, as Frith continues, however genuine his identification with the socially unprivileged, and however well his music plugs the gap produced by frustrated aspirations, his act is a fabricated solution to the problems he outlines. This is because his ability to pitch what Frith calls 'rural truth against urban deceit', and to 'pioneer values against bureaucratic routines' is harnessed to the corporate success of mass sales.[28] Alienation, loneliness and feelings of insignificance, this is to say, cannot be overcome by the very same mechanisms that produce them. Hence, even though Frith is open to the tradition of populism in the USA and free of bourgeois nostalgia, he finds nonetheless, like Adorno, that the culture industry provides malady and remedy in the same bottle.[29]

Frith tackles the question of value by making a distinction between escapist and transformative, or empowering, musics. He writes:

> Culture as transformation . . . must challenge experience, must be difficult, must be *unpopular*. There are, in short, political as well as sociological and aesthetic reasons for challenging populism. The problem is how to do this while appreciating the popular, taking it seriously on its own terms. And I know this is where my own tastes will inform everything else that follows, my own tastes, that is, for the *unpopular popular*, my own belief that the 'difficult' appeals through the traces it carries of another world in which it would be 'easy'. The utopian impulse, the *negation* of everyday life, the aesthetic impulse that Adorno recognized in high art, must be part of low art too.[30]

This nod to Adorno is dependent on the idea, if not the actual discourses, of the 'magic that can set you free' rock argument. It jettisons the spurious notion of community, but envisages music that, notwithstanding its commodity status, defies standardization and surely looks beyond the administered world. While exposing the illusions of rock beliefs, therefore, Frith retains from these discourses the idea of a critical impulse and indicates that the rock myth is about more than subculture. His response to John Lennon's death, for example, argues that Lennon sought to work in commercial music without being governed by the culture of stardom.[31] The comment suggests that music can operate within the mechanisms of mass production and reception while pointing beyond them.

For me, music derives value from a capacity to articulate its constituent discourses, thereby enabling people to enter into dialogue with these positions and, perhaps, link them to experiences more closely associated with their own lives. How does a major figure such as Bob Dylan measure up to this model? One cannot answer this question without considering the identity that Dylan invented for himself to hide a middle-class background. Two things are striking here: one, that Dylan needed this persona; two, that its authenticity is somehow considered to affect the value of his music. From a sympathetic perspective, one can see that Dylan probably wanted to identify personally with the stories he narrated, and that this involvement was part of the creative process. To consider him a fake on account of an invented past demands, rather narrowly, that his authorial voice should marry with the details of his life. Dylan is of course not exempt from the Springsteen irony that a slice of reality is big business, but his songs, particularly from the 1960s, voice critical social practices that are not easily silenced by huge sales. Put differently, the songs and social movements which they embody form a 'common disposition of energy and direction', to use the now familiar phrase by Raymond Williams.[32] Something of this disposition of energy and direction is held like a time capsule in these songs, even when they are heard in less politically charged times.

A successful album such as *Blood on the Tracks* cannot be described as unpopular, quite the reverse; but it is not populist because its themes of frustrated love and wistful memories retain a degree of awkwardness in their delivery that is not easily removed.[33] Its motifs of broken relationships and poignant memories function on more than one level: firstly, released in 1975, the album coincides with a reflexive stage in the history of rock, which by then had a tradition to consider; secondly, many of the tracks revisit earlier songs and thereby reconfigure Dylan's career – 'If you see her, say hello', for example, evokes 'Girl from the North Country', from *The Freewheelin' Bob Dylan*.[34] The intimate tone of *Blood on the Tracks*, which contrasts with the apocalyptic topics of the protest songs, enables a more delicate voice to emerge, sometimes by entwining the lyrics around a female character.[35]

'If you see her' finds Dylan assuming the possessive character normally attributed to women, while considering his lover's need for freedom. The arpeggiated accompaniment creates the fullness that the voice pines for. The grain of Dylan's lonely vocals rubs against this richness, enacting the sense of loss and separation, and creating what might be called a modernist dissonance by refusing to be beautifully absorbed in the music. Such disparities are also found in the lyrics, with the lines about replaying scenes that went by so fast presenting the same events as both fleeting moments and over-rehearsed memories.[36] Transient and unreconciled, the cliché lurking in these sentiments is unsettled and captures the mood of the song. Perhaps it also encrypts the dilemma of an ageing rock movement that harks to a memory of immediacy, but knows this, too, was never quite as recalled.

For a more abrasive exposure of the rock community's pretensions, we should turn to punk rock. If punk is not the end of rock it is sometimes seen to be, it remains a significant intervention, lambasting rock's ostentation by celebrating a lack of technique and eliminating expressive claims through its alienating stylistic bricolage. Targeting in particular the middle-class values of progressive rock, punk rejected attempts to combine art music innovation with the energy of rock. Furthermore, it confronted an ageing rock generation, increasingly disenchanted with the ideology it had once relished, whose songs of rebellion, sexual liberation and social concern were taken up in the late 1970s by advertising campaigns targeted at people now interested in wine coolers, executive cars and personal insurance.[37] In this environment punk announced the end of a dominant rock ideology.

By exposing the commodity character of rock, punk opened the way for understanding music as constructed image. As the ideology of rock shrivelled, so popular music became more openly organized by free-market pluralism.[38] However, the decline of rock was not geographically even: in the 1980s rock occupied a less dominant position in Britain and the United States, but became a significant genre in eastern Europe, particularly in the former German Democratic Republic, where it became associated with the political protest and struggle that resulted in the dismantling of the Berlin Wall.[39] In this capacity, it carried many of the meanings that had been jettisoned in the West. Meanwhile in its former strongholds, rock became a style amongst others and the boundaries between genres became more fluid. In this sense rock shares the trajectory of new music: both have declined as dominant institutions under conditions of postmodernism and both have become enclaves that coexist alongside other musics.

Clearly we have travelled a long way from Sharpe's and Lloyd's attempts to construct a folk community. We have seen that even though rock is an urban music of the type that folk ideals resist, it too tried to establish itself as something authentic, that is to say, as something that is not dominated by the market. This ideology now looks like a historical construction, as does the typically male self-expression that rock embodies. Of course all culture and cultural criticism is also historically constructed, so rock is not unique in this sense. An enriched understanding of rock does not, therefore, invalidate everything that happened in its name; it enables us, rather, to be less tied by the dominant codes of rock, but still able to appreciate rock, or any other music, that can reflect on its own social codes. Since punk revealed rock's generalized oppositional stance to be less compelling than once thought, theory has become more aware of the identities and spaces that musics occupy, and this positioning is the topic of the next section.

Perspectives

Frith and Angela McRobbie introduced the sociology of popular music to sexual politics when they attempted to analyse gender roles in pop. Frith has subsequently acknowledged that the principal shortcoming of 'Rock and Sexuality' (published in 1978) is its tendency to essentialize sexuality by describing rock as music about sexuality, rather than understanding it as a discourse through which sexuality is constructed.[40] His later opinion is that sexual energy is expressed through codes that create conventions of sexuality rather than reflecting existing behaviours from elsewhere. Indeed music and theory have certainly moved on since the original article was written, but despite well-documented criticisms it remains a useful starting place for discussion of gender construction in popular music.

Writing in the context of the 1970s, the authors identify two strands of popular music, associated, respectively, with masculine and feminine gender constructions, which they name as 'cock rock' and 'teenybop'. These stereotypes are produced not only by male bands, but by a male-dominated industry, extending its priorities to all levels of production. A performance style that signifies masculine sexuality can be traced back to the mannerisms of 1950s rock 'n' roll (stylized in Elvis Presley's celebrated gyrations) and leads to stereotypical displays of male sexuality.[41] In the case of 1970s rock, these took the form of plunging shirts, tight trousers, and crude sexual gestures, matched by thrusting rhythms and musical climaxes. Writing about Thin Lizzy, Frith and McRobbie comment: 'the music is loud, rhythmically insistent, built around techniques of arousal and climax; the lyrics are assertive and arrogant, though the exact words are less significant than the vocal styles involved, the shouting and screaming'.[42] Such macho imagery not only forges masculinity, it also creates a passive feminine other by contrasting the 'freedom' symbolized in its stylized abandonment to a possessive female sexuality.

Unlike masculinist rock, teenybop is perceived to be about romance and emotion, expressed in non-sexualized terms, with its stars portrayed as men that need support and sympathy. Unlike the public space of the rock venue, the forum in which girls typically listen to such music tends to be the bedroom with other friends. These circumstances lead Frith and McRobbie to conclude as follows: 'The vision of freedom on which these girls are drawing is a vision of the freedom to be individual wives, mothers, lovers, of the freedom to be glamorous, desirable male sex objects.'[43] McRobbie's (1980) feminist critique of subcultural theory, which discusses Hebdige in particular, also dwells on the environment in which girls experience music.[44] Acknowledging the importance of Hebdige's work, especially on punk, she points out that it theorizes a primarily male experience. Building on this, she notes that its oppositional culture of bricolage and shock is based on a street culture reluctant to acknowledge the domestic environment that feeds and maintains such activity.

A focus, like this, on the ways in which music is consumed inevitably leads away from the production process to the active participation of fans in creating meaning. Writing later, Frith comments, 'what is interesting now is not how the objects of desire are made and sold – as pinups, heroines, stars – but how sexual subjectivity works, how we use popular music and imagery to understand what it means to have desires, to be desirable'.[45] It is as well to remember, however, that the active reception envisaged here is likely to be facilitated by songs and interpretive communities in which the subject positions, whether of the song, the singer, or the listener, are not overdetermined, since rigidly enforced identity tends to produce either conformity or rejection with little else in between.

Heavy metal is just such a genre in which gender codes are generally overdetermined, making creative interpretation that much harder. Taking his cue from John Fiske's analysis of the way masculinity is depicted on TV, Robert Walser argues that metal, particularly in the 1980s, responds to a dilemma in which patriarchal society produces dominant images of masculinity, but deprives men of the social power required to realize them. Metal fans tend to be socially and economically underprivileged (and until recently almost entirely male), thus the metal scene fantasy (which repeats many of the gestures Frith and McRobbie describe) enables them to recoup the power of masculinity they are otherwise denied. Femininity constitutes a problem for this ideology because it suggests a loss of power, therefore it is frequently excluded through homosocial bonding and protected identities. Recently, however, with more female metal fans (and some performers), women have been able to participate in its power fantasies and thereby counteract the effects of social subordination through traditionally masculine codes. When women appropriate an enforced masculine identity, the latter's inbuilt fear of the feminine does not of course vanish, but it may be redirected. Walser suggests, for instance, that when women collect and exchange glossy pictures of metal stars they are not necessarily absorbing dominant rules, but using the images as a medium through which to negotiate gender identity and form friendships.[46]

The rigid masculine tropes employed by metal are sociologically significant but remain dubious constructions of subjectivity. Elsewhere, the claims of core identity are rather more compelling and access directly the dilemmas of authenticity and essentialism. Nowhere are these issues more sensitive than in debates about black music. A popular view considers that black music, notably jazz, is somehow more natural, its rhythmic dimension more in tune with the body, than other musics, particularly when compared with the European art tradition. This notion nourishes a familiar mind/body binary that occurs in much cultural debate, and is already familiar from the modernist/popular divide. At one level this distinction can be attributed to a difference between a participatory African music and a European art music tied to a history of aesthetic contemplation. However, these are insufficient grounds from which to conclude either that the body is absent in European classical music or that African music lacks complexity. Underlying this binary divide is the ideology that the body and movement flow directly into music, unmediated by convention. Derrida's reading of Rousseau, we have seen, suggests that a comparable difference between a natural, oral mode of communication and an artificial, written mode cannot be maintained, since the former is itself a set of conventions. Applying this perspective to black music, we find that musical immediacy relies on learned associations between musical configurations and the body. This is not to deny that there is a somatic dimension to, say, reggae, or to suggest it is artificial, but to observe that this, too, is fashioned through a set of social practices.

Established procedures are also apparent when we try to identify a set of characteristics that are particular to black music. Philip Tagg argues that features such as blue notes, call-and-response patterns, syncopation and improvisation, often considered intrinsic to black music, are all found in other musical traditions, though in different configurations. Antiphonal psalm singing, for example, has a long history in both Europe and the Middle East.[47] This said, features such as dialogical exchange and layered repetition do characterize much black music, but they are always embedded in cultural practices, signifying particular experiences and locations. If we take the music of James Brown, that habitus is the African-American struggle for power. David Brackett's analysis of Brown's 'Superbad' (recorded in 1971) indicates that paradigmatic substitution plays an important role in this song because the lyrics are a game with formulaic phrases, chosen more for their sound than their linear coherence.[48] Together with a comparable series of melodic substitutions that make up the music's phrases, the song construction frustrates European narrative expectations. Additionally, the groove (rhythmic scheme) is also built through combinations of small units, which combine to form larger configurations, in a transmutation of West African polymetric practice that signifies a particular culture. Combining timbre and harmony into this schema, Brackett argues that the Afro-American sense of this music emerges on several levels through reference to codes associated with black culture and politics.

Brackett's account manages to find a way between the Charybdis of essentializing black music as a domain of somatic freedom and the Scylla of emptying its encultured meaning. Paul Gilroy has also proposed an interesting way through this dilemma by envisaging a culture that is not restricted to being African, American, Caribbean or British, since it can address the common experiences of all of these. His name for this grouping is the black Atlantic and he positions it within the discourses of modernity, instead of presenting it as a field of immediacy that lies outside this sphere. Consequently, his model of black identity avoids reducing the complexity of cultural interaction to a single pattern. Speaking of music, he says 'my point here is that the unashamedly hybrid character of these black Atlantic cultures continually confounds any simplistic (essentialist or anti-essentialist) understanding of the relationship between racial identity and racial non-identity, between folk cultural authenticity and pop cultural betrayal'.[49]

One effect of this hybridity is that it skews what Gilroy calls the Afrocentric idea of Africa as the only cultural resource for black music. As an example of west to east cultural flow, he cites a speech given by Nelson Mandela in Detroit (1990) in which he recalls that he listened to Motown, the sound of Detroit as he called it, during his long jail sentence.[50] Another effect of hybridity is that it exposes black music to multiple influences that blur cultural boundaries and potentially dissolve hard-won identities. Hybridity-talk overcomes rigid subject positions by showing how they are constructed and hence might be reconstructed. But it can also relativize racial identity by reducing it to a set of conventions of no more significance than any other. In these circumstances hybridity-talk can encourage a shop-window approach to cultural differences, where identities are not only flexibly negotiated, they can also be modelled and tried, consumed and passed over like other commodities.[51]

The result is a typically postmodernist combination of personas and styles, as found in the work of Madonna. She has been likened to a corporation that produces images of herself in various media,[52] thereby repudiating the non-commercial claims of rock authenticity. Instead of trying to embody a particular identity, as most rock performers typically do, she slips in and out of subject positions from song to song and within songs, notably in 'Express Yourself', where she engages in multiple subject positions.[53] For many commentators this flexible subject positioning offers resources for softening gender stereotyping, and much discussion of Madonna has focused on her dismantling of the virgin/whore binary that polarizes female sexuality between extremes. Using imagery from both sides of the binary, argue Fiske and Susan McClary, she corresponds to neither. The crucifix in 'Like a Prayer', for example, is worn by an overtly sexual woman, thus breaking its usual pattern of signification. Madonna offers to the teenage girls that consume her music the opportunity to construct subjectivity along lines other than the dominant stereotypes offered by patriarchal society. By parodying gender models and their construction, she gains control of her own image, and once in possession of these codes can subvert them: if codes are constructed, she seems to say, then they can be reconstructed. In 'Cherish' the fluid subjectivity normally attributed to women through mermaid fantasies is transferred to aquatic men who reveal whales' tails as they frolic in the surf, while Madonna's shoreline routine includes a muscular pose.

Fiske's evaluation of Madonna serves to exemplify a strand of contemporary cultural studies, showing the departures that have occurred since the work outlined earlier in this chapter. Talking of Madonna's feminine and Catholic imagery, he comments:

> The products are purified into signifiers; their ideological signifieds are dumped and left behind in their original context. These freed signifieds do

> not necessarily mean *something*, they do not necessarily acquire new signifieds. Rather, the act of freeing them from their ideological context signifies their users' freedom from that context. It signifies the power (however hard the struggle to attain it) of the subordinate to exert some control in the cultural process of making meanings.[54]

Whatever the value of freeing symbols from their signifying context and plunging them into multiple and conflicting signification, the notion of no signification, signifiers without signifieds, is perplexing, silly even. It is allied to the idea, envisioned by some postmodernist theorists, that resistance, no matter to what, is inherently valuable, and is characterized by a refusal to engage any positioned subjectivity at all.

In a critical discussion of postmodernism's evaluation of Madonna, Susan Bordo comments, 'what is celebrated is a continual creative escape from containment, location and definition',[55] a way of saying we are offered an impossibility because a view can only be a view from somewhere. The implication is that the dominant images of hierarchy are so strong that they even govern fantasies of escape, as if the industrial boss in 'Express Yourself' were merely a subject style unrelated to the authority that exerts control on other people's lives. Granted these videos are fantasies, not models for political transformation, but they leave a huge gap between the identities they parade and the circumstances that control people's lives. We are left wondering whether Madonna is the author or product of the codes she offers.

So far, like most reception of Madonna's music-videos, I have discussed the images more than the music. Nevertheless, music-video is a multimedia genre in which meaning is constructed through intersecting strands, not by visual images alone. As mentioned in Chapter 2, film music works largely through semiotic associations, which tend to fill out the narrative or sometimes counterpoint it. Music-video is different in that the images are usually added to an already complete song. This fact has led Andrew Goodwin to comment that video images take their meaning from the semiotic implications of the music.[56] In a circular process, he is saying that certain images strengthen the associations of a particular music, which then signifies those images. And this is true of Madonna's videos where the dance music, not surprisingly, signifies the stylized dancing that she and others engage in, while the medium depends on leaving behind everyday concerns and entering a fantasy realm. Furthermore, the images of that arena are often taken from film, with a particular look signifying a particular type of film. 'Material Girl' references Marilyn Monroe in *Gentlemen Prefer Blondes*, for example, and 'Express Yourself' has the look of Fritz Lang's *Metropolis*.

The music of 'Material Girl' matches the video to the extent that since it makes no pretence to be anything other than commercial dance music, it fits the material world Madonna sings about and enacts, where 'the boy with the cold hard cash is always Mister Right'.[57] The dance track does not, however, obviously reference Marilyn Monroe, and interacts ambiguously with the second visual narrative strand concerned with the film producer who offers Madonna daisies and whisks her away in a hired pickup truck. On one level this thread contradicts the materialism of the song, on another confirms it since the producer is unlikely to be poor, despite his gestures.

This brings us back to the theme of how multiple signifiers are scattered across multimedia. So much writing on Madonna celebrates disrupted narratives and subverted codes that we tend to forget that her music obeys standard pop procedures and is not particularly fragmented. Significantly, it is these procedures that determine the cutting rhythm of the video in 'Material Girl', so that we switch images as the music moves from verse to chorus or from phrase to phrase.[58] The outcome is that the narrative disjunctions are at least partly attributable to the musical scheme, which is in itself not particularly heterogeneous. Consequently, what looks like open signification on the image level is controlled by structured signification on another level that makes Fiske's celebration of floating signifiers less credulous.

Nor are multiple subject positions obligatory to loosen gender codes. Even within a conservative institution such as country and western, it is possible for performers to engage with the practices that define their genre. Typically, these are based on a construction of rural America, which never existed, in which men are strong and resourceful, women weak and dependent. But even tough living provides room for manoeuvre. It is reasonable to claim, for instance, that Dolly Parton is in control of the big-hair image of femininity she represents. The songs she performs, many written by her, convey familiar themes of loss, betrayal and survival (things that other people did to her), but in the best cases, the conventions do not simply describe these themes, they performatively construct them: the work they do is part of their meaning, hence they become less restrictive and more open to interpretation. Frith notes the irony of Parton's control in her songs of dependence, but his view that these songs 'display vocal skill rather than an emotional state' is confusing.[59] It would be more accurate to say that the emotional assurance her voice conveys is not always congruent with the lyric sentiments she sings. In probably her best-known song, 'I will always love you', the sentiments of an incomplete person, releasing the person she will always love from containment, is conveyed in the spoken section, but contradicted by the vocal power of the chorus, which provides the assurance the words deny.[60]

k.d. lang's third album, *Absolute Torch and Twang*, is celebrated for resignifying country gender roles, particularly masculine, cowboy imagery. For lang, it is the humorous twang of country music that enables its meanings to be reworked. In Martha Mockus's words, 'for lang, to restore, or uncloset, the "real humor or twang" of country music is to engage with a camp musical strategy'.[61] 'Pullin' back the reins', from this album, employs an ungendered 'I–You' mode of address,[62] exploring an indeterminacy that enables the listener to gender the medium for him or herself. The sentiments and lyrics employ outdoor cowboy imagery: love came out of nowhere, a 'gust of wind / brushed my hair and kissed my skin', and these words create a tension between purpose and abandon when heard alongside the chorus, 'pullin' back the reins / trying to remain / tall in the saddle'.[63] The song suggests yielding to something as 'wild and free' as the country in which the narrative is set. Its music gives way to a slow pulse with upbeats accenting beats 1 and 3, and is characterized by the IV to I motion of the introduction and the flattened-third riff heard here and in the bridge. lang's voice is strong and sensual, with a good range of colour, while the relationship she describes is suggested in the dialogue between her vocal slides and the enticing voice of the twangy lead guitar. When this album was released in 1989, lang had yet to come out publicly as a lesbian, but had nevertheless attracted a large lesbian following who understood the meaning of an androgynous style of dress, short hair, and the implicit tropes used in her songs. It was not, therefore, just her own style that constructed her public persona, it was also the way her fans read her.

The discussion of gender in Chapter 3 talked about how authorial intention might be dispersed by performance and reception strategies, noting that when women singers hold the stage, they temporarily displace the composer and acquire authorial presence. In much popular music there is not a flagged songwriter to displace (since pop is produced, like other contemporary commodities, by interactions between teams and technology), therefore performers, particularly lead singers, procure that role even more easily than in opera. Furthermore, it is generally assumed that a singer embodies personalized emotions when performing a song. Music-video can either concentrate that impression by providing images of performed emotion or dilute it by associating the music with imagery that draws attention away from its performers. If a vocal protagonist is dispensed with, of course, then music is identified less strongly with a particular character. (Arguably, the machine-driven British dance music of the 1990s facilitates a dispersed subjectivity in which dancers respond to each other, rather than collectively acting out a single identity,[64] though the volume and fast pulse rule out more contemplative moods.) The dominion that performers exert on the production of their music obviously varies, but it is likely that singers perceived to be strongly in control of their identity (even when performing cover versions) will exert more influence on the process than those reproducing standard conventions. It is hard to imagine, for example, that lang's intervention in country would have been possible without her exerting considerable authority on all aspects of production.

When we talk of asserting control over identity, it is worth remembering that identity is thoroughly socialized and that sounds themselves are part of this socialization. So when we assemble through sounds an identity, however individual, we draw on non-individualized social codes of music through which we interact with others. Frith conveys this process when he writes of 'a coming together of the sensual, the emotional, and the social as performance', adding that 'music doesn't represent values but lives them'.[65] However, his accompanying suggestion that these qualities are somehow opposed to meaning and interpretation is less helpful: surely the values music lives is what it means, since meaning is not restricted to static interpretation of fixed texts. Elsewhere, he effectively combines a sense of music as socialized performance with a utopian streak. Modifying his language, we can talk of popular music simultaneously negating and reconfiguring the everyday, thereby modelling social transformation.[66] By hearing differentiated subject positions where Adorno only encountered conformity, we find meaning in the everyday.

5 Places

Western attitudes towards music from elsewhere in the world can be addressed in two ways: firstly, by examining how the West studies non-Western cultures and, secondly, by considering how Western music conveys musics of other cultures. Habitually, musicology studies Western music, while non-Western musics are the preserve of ethnomusicology, though the latter is defined as much by its ethnological interests as by the musics it studies. The study of non-Western influences on Western music, meanwhile, might be described as an amalgam of musicology and orientalism. Early work on orientalism concentrated on portrayals of those regions deemed to be oriental – particularly the Middle East – in Western literature, and has developed into a field known as post-colonial studies, which focuses on writings from previously colonized territories. A comparable shift is also to be found in what we might call post-colonial musicology, which touches on ethnomusicology as the borders between Western and non-Western cultures weaken, particularly as popular music becomes increasingly porous to world music.

Orientalism

Post-colonial studies build on the pioneering work undertaken in Edward Said's *Orientalism*, which appeared in 1978. *Orientalism* is significant for using the interpretive resources of critical theory to study constructions of race and ethnicity, thereby turning theory away from its Eurocentric preoccupations. Said's position, which is indebted to Michel Foucault, is that occidental responses to the Orient, whether aesthetic, scholarly or economic, cannot be separated from the configurations of power deriving from the domination of oriental peoples. This perspective has been very influential, though it has also been criticized for overgeneralizing the homogeneity of colonial power.[1] Western discourses of the East, it turns out, have more to say about the West than the East, which functions as something like an unconscious: a place where impulses that are not acknowledged in Western symbolic values can be located. As Bart Moore-Gilbert puts it, 'the East is characteristically produced in Orientalist discourse as – variously – voiceless, sensual, female, despotic, irrational and backward. By contrast, the West is represented as masculine, democratic, rational, moral, dynamic and progressive'.[2] (This binary construction is not dissimilar to the one discussed in Chapter 3 in which music appears as a feminine, irrational other to the disciplined masculinist subject.)

Nineteenth-century depictions of the Middle East, whether in literature, art or music, contribute to stereotyped models of gender and ethnicity, typically portraying voluptuous, available women and cruel, despotic men.[3] Such attitudes are found in music, especially opera, when we view it as a product of a culture built on certain perceptions of the East. Saint-Saëns's opera *Samson et Dalila,* for instance, rests on an archetypal East–West binary opposition. As Ralph Locke puts it, 'Samson, the proto-European, is male and favoured by God; Delilah, chief representative of the East, is female and seeks his downfall and that of the God-chosen West.'[4] The Orient, depicted as female, is clearly something that weakens male resolve, in this conception, and is to be resisted. Delilah's seductive powers are at their height, not surprisingly, in the love scene (Act II), where, Locke argues, Delilah exhibits genuine desire for Samson, despite her later betrayal, of a directness that would not be associated with a European character of social standing. The two ballets, the 'Dance of the Priestesses of Dagon' (Act I) and the Bacchanale (Act III) provide the most conventional musical evocations of Eastern sensuality by using established signifiers of the exotic, notably the repeated augmented second featured in the Bacchanale (see Ex. 3). And this musical feature feeds into the more widespread orientalism of the opera, Locke suggests, 'heightening rather than bridging the dichotomous gap between self and other'.[5]

In *Culture and Imperialism,* a collection of essays published after *Orientalism,* Said turns his attention not only to post-colonial writers but also to orientalist opera, namely Verdi's *Aida*. He prefaces this section by outlining his aims: principally, to show that the categories by which European art is normally discussed, such as 'genre, periodization, nationality, or style', are irradiated by the worldly

Ex. 3

pursuits of power, authority, privilege, and dominance, a structure of attitude and reference that was in place before the officially designated age of empire.[6] Since *Aida* is set in Egypt, stages a dance of Moorish slaves and features death by asphyxiation beneath a temple, it is not hard to read as an orientalist opera. Verdi was commissioned to write it for the new opera house in Cairo (the performance took place in 1871), which was situated on the divide between the European and Muslim sectors of the city. It was intended as entertainment that would reinforce the attitudes of the European population who administered Egypt as part of a quasi-European empire. Its librettist was Auguste Mariette, a Frenchman principally known as an archaeologist associated with the fashion for European universal expositions. The image of Egypt that Mariette presented in these displays was of an ancient civilization, viewed through imperialist eyes, that had little to do with modern life in Egypt. This attitude passed into the libretto, Said argues, and since Verdi had no particular interest in Egypt, ancient or modern, he used its ancient associations as a screen on which to project his own imagination.

Musical exoticism in *Aida*, as in *Samson et Dalila*, is a facet of the overall orientalist conception. The prime examples of recognizably orientalist music are the chanting of the priestess (Act I, scene 2) and the following sacred dance. On a broader spectrum, the scene in Amneris's chamber in Act II, in which she torments Aida, combines orientalist themes of cruelty and sensuality, while the triumphal march (also Act II) provides the opportunity to experience otherness as spectacle (a scene seized upon in Wieland Wagner's 1960s production, which presented the Ethiopian prisoners as an ethnographic exhibit in a prehistoric vision of Africa). Moving away from specifically exotic moments to the overall conception, Said concludes: '*Aida* can be enjoyed and interpreted as a kind of curatorial art, whose rigour and unbending frame recall, with relentlessly mortuary logic, a precise historical moment and a specifically dated aesthetic form, an imperial spectacle designed to alienate and impress an almost exclusively European audience.'[7]

This perspective is both endorsed and challenged by Paul Robinson, who relates the subject matter of *Aida* to the tradition of Verdi's nationalism, forged in protest at the Austrian domination of Italy.[8] *Aida*, Robinson argues, casts the Egyptians as European-style oppressors and aligns Verdi's sympathies with the oppressed Ethiopians. This interpretation has some credibility, despite its dependence on authorial intention and biography, but does not seriously dent Said's analysis, which extends beyond the narrative message to the ways the opera is criss-crossed by colonialist discourses. Even if the Egyptians do play an imperialist role in the opera, the sense of a museum culture is still present, affecting both the Egyptians and the Ethiopians.

By the onset of the twentieth century, it became clear that the timeless qualities of the Middle East were a fantasy, a projection of Western attitudes (seeking shelter from the pressures of modernity) that were not really attached to any location.[9] An example of this faux-orientalism, Kramer argues, can be found in Ravel's *Daphnis et Chloé*. Kramer presents Ravel's technological advances through a constellation (reminiscent of Walter Benjamin's *Arcades Project*) of commerce, consumption and exoticism that he finds embodied in a postcard depicting cosmopolitan shopping at a turn-of-the-century Parisian bazaar. The exoticism that Europeans had found in their colonies, the postcard suggests, is governed by the image of the commodity form as something to consume in an age when department stores were offering rich spectacles of merchandise. Likewise, the modernism of Ravel's *fin de siècle* technique is used to capture the archaism of Arcadian Greece in a display of what Kramer calls conspicuous sublimation. And he pursues the commodity deeper into Ravel's score: neither static nor dynamic and governed by techniques of 'reproduction, iteration and similitude,' he argues, 'the music expands to fill what might be called the temporality of display'.[10] The result is a depthless music that unfolds cinematically with structure serving to disseminate colour and texture, reversing the binary distinction between depth and surface that places the former in the centre and the latter at the margins.

Ravel's consumptionist ethos prompts Kramer to end with the following statement: 'Both the means and the end of the dream of mass consumption is the acquisition of pleasure in material form. But the pleasure acquired is dematerialized in the very process of acquisition. It is always, and of necessity, purely imaginary.'[11] Like the commodity form, therefore, Ravel's music (in a deliberate aesthetic programme) is a simulacrum because it is divorced from production – a phantasmagoric surface offering a vision of plenitude and bliss it cannot deliver. Earlier in the chapter, following Miriam Hansen, Kramer brings out the paradox of consumerism in less quixotic fashion. 'On the one hand', he argues, 'it unsettles social hierarchies, normalizes abundance rather than scarcity, and promotes the continuous exchange of work for pleasure. On the other hand, it colonizes not only dependent nations and classes but also the subjectivity of the consumer, which becomes identified with the need for continual expenditure.'[12] Could not a similar point be made about postmodernism? The amalgam of consumption and orientalism certainly touches on the dilemmas of postmodernism, which are indelibly stamped by the global market we now inhabit. On the one hand, postmodernism releases us from traditions and ingrained habits, offering liberating alternatives; on the other hand, it cannot deliver the fulfilment suggested by the multitudinous identities it offers for consumption.

I shall return to this dilemma in Chapter 6; for now we can consider the fate of orientalism later in the twentieth century. The mid-century doctrine of formalism did not encourage the displays of colour and surface for their own sake found in *Daphnis et Chloé*, and orientalism's proximity to popular culture further reduced its prospects. Instead of seeking to offer displays of otherness in music, later composers sought to integrate textures and procedures from distant musics into their own languages. Olivier Messiaen's use of Indian scales, for example, is clearly conceived in a constructionist aesthetic, though his mysticism retains something of the fantasy element of orientalism. An example of the latter tendency is to be found in the 'Jardin du sommeil d'amour' movement from the *Turangalîla-Symphonie*, with its dream-world garden of love, offering a geographically vague exoticism.

John Cage, meanwhile, presents a contrasting, multi-faceted, Japanese-inspired orientalism that draws on non-Western ideas and sounds. His Zen Buddhism rejects modernity's fixation on progress, while his use, for example, of Japanese temple gongs in the *First Construction (in Metal)*, of 1939, expands the sound palette of Western music. But this Zen-based application of chance techniques to composition is more indicative of modernism than an invocation of non-Western subjectivity. The chance operations it allows him to perform mirror the experience of subjectivity in a system-driven society, indifferent to individual aspirations. Still, by turning subjectivity in unexpected directions, Cage may well have made some headway in breaking down rigid divisions between Western and non-Western outlooks. Since the Western subject no longer occupies the centre point in his music, it cannot function as the norm against which other world-views appear exotic. The downside to his anonymous procedures is that they fragment all subjectivity, so that although the normal/other binary is dissolved, no identity is encountered in a particularly specific manner. If, post-Cage, we are able to be less suspicious of subjectivity, while increasing our knowledge of how it is constructed, then music can embody both affinity and difference without having to attribute sensuality to another realm.

Ethnomusicology

In contrast to the orientalist tendency to project Western fantasies onto other cultures, ethnomusicology seeks to understand music as experienced by its participants. In so doing, of course, it also encounters the problems of self and other. My aim in the following section is to show how such pressures, already familiar from other areas of musicology, exert themselves in ethnomusicology. Alan Merriam's description of ethnomusicology as 'the study of music in culture' extends its remit to all music,[13] including that of the West, thereby challenging binary distinctions between 'normal' and 'other' musics. The problem with this formula is that it implies that music and culture have somehow to be brought together. For this reason, the definition quickly became 'the study of music as culture', overcoming any sense of music and culture as separate entities.[14] The study of music as culture is a good depiction of the recent shifts that have taken place in musicology as a whole.

The current vogue for contesting premisses, methodologies and disciplinary aims has long been a staple activity of ethnomusicology. Its researchers typically devote much space to establishing the aims and claims of the material presented, unlike those historical musicologists who could once present their findings in an environment of stable methodology. The epistemological uncertainty that now pervades musicology, therefore, might be understood as a more widespread application of the dilemmas that are familiar to ethnomusicology. The originality that some recent musicology attributes to itself not only dismisses modernism in a generalized fashion, it also passes over the innovatory cultural work that has taken place in ethnomusicology. Kay Kaufman Shelemay expresses the latter sentiment as follows: 'I am delighted that "new musicology" has moved full force to considerations of music and culture, but I marvel at the oversight of decades of ethnomusicological scholarship long concerned with these themes.'[15] It would not, however, be appropriate to rush to the conclusion that musicology has simply caught up with ethnomusicology. For one thing, the latter has not been free of the positivist and formalist excesses that beset musicology; for another, the reflexive transformations that musicology has undergone, as we have seen, derive from many sources, not all of which have the specifically anthropological flavour of ethnomusicology.

The intellectual heritage of ethnomusicology is a combination of three streams: comparative musicology (which is concerned with studying all musics and has roots in Adler's model), anthropology (which is preoccupied with ethnological investigation), and national folklore movements (which seek to preserve and disseminate heritage). Therefore ethnomusicology's affinities with other strands of musicology owe more to a shared subject matter than to a shared methodology. Nevertheless, since ethnomusicologists more often work in music departments than in anthropology departments, they sit, somewhat precariously, between the usually historical, sometimes sociological, interests of musicology, and the more obviously ethnological concerns of anthropology, with different individuals leaning nearer to one side than the other. Anthropological study of music does not, of course, restrict itself to non-Western musics; its remit extends to all musics. Ethnomusicology's focus is on lived experience in the present, on how it feels to inhabit a particular tradition, with participatory fieldwork a key method of research.[16] Like most humanities and social science disciplines, anthropology has been affected by postmodernist values, and these have led it to question whether the study of 'other' societies is a form of colonialism and, consequently, to seek a more dialogic relationship with the peoples it observes.

Shadowing this development, Timothy Rice suggests that ethnomusicology has moved through three stages, progressing, he writes, 'from a concern with historical and evolutionary questions in its early "comparative musicology" stage to a concern for music in social life after [Merriam's] *The Anthropology of Music*, to a concern for the individual in history and society in the most recent or next phase'.[17] Rice's stages do not entirely correspond to developments elsewhere in musicology, but the recent turn to identity politics is recognizable. And both disciplines have been influenced by the insistence of anthropologist Clifford Geerz that individual human actions can only be understood through an embedding cultural context, to be represented by what he calls 'thick description'. Applying this criterion to musicology, Gary Tomlinson argues 'that musical art works are the codifications or inscribed reflections of human creative actions', hence they too require thick cultural interpretation.[18] The result is that the narrow range in which Western music is traditionally studied expands to include dense webs of signification.

Anthropologically derived approaches to musicology dispute the essentializing of music as object, whether this occurs within the Western tradition of scholarship or as an imposition of Western text-based models of knowledge on societies who do not objectify music in the same way. By transcribing and recording music, and by producing articles and books, ethnomusicologists translate oral traditions and socialized performances into forms to be dissected – into items that can be placed in a library in a format that is deemed to be knowledge. Another way of putting this is to say that an integrated, socialized way of life must be transcribed into another configuration if it is to be accepted by Western notions of knowledge. When, for example, an oral tradition such as Inuit music is transcribed, the normative procedures of a notational system are imposed onto a music that is not understood in this way by its practitioners. Even if the transcription is executed with sensitivity, and even if important features such as quality of vocal tone, which cannot be transcribed, are acknowledged, a vehicle of social interaction is reduced to an abstract spatial system that is derived from, in most cases, tonal models.[19] In effect, notation makes the performance something that can be understood as a museum piece, freezing its tissue into a fixed configuration.

This said, ethnomusicologists are well aware of these hazards and seek to represent the musical understanding of participants, rather than impose external criteria. And we have seen that it is not just oral traditions that are affected by crystallization, since Western notated music is also dependent on performance practices. The score of a

Beethoven symphony, for instance, assumes an orchestral tradition without which it would make little sense. When analytic or editorial work focuses entirely on a score, therefore, it only addresses one dimension of the music.

Western attitudes can inform even the most well-intentioned acts. To describe a particular social activity as music is to impose an aesthetic classification characteristic of Western art-music traditions, which is by no means of universal validity. When, for example, native Australians undertake a religious ceremony, it is not for them necessarily broken down into components such as music, dance and prayer; therefore to take one such component and call it 'music' is to impose a frame that is not recognized by the participants. This said, a learning process must start from somewhere. By deploying a familiar aesthetic, a listener can gain access to a less familiar one and in the process modify the original listening strategy. In this way a communicative process is set in motion that can negotiate between differing cultural perspectives. Even if a view from somewhere happens to peer from the shelter of bourgeois music, it can at least try to encounter the strangeness of a different perspective.

Philip Bohlman gives an example of how widely perceptions of musical ownership can vary, noting that in dominant societies music can be bought in the forms of artefacts such as CDs or scores. For North American Flathead Indians, on the other hand, he writes, 'it is the experience of dreaming the song, not the song itself, that distinguishes it as belonging to an individual'.[20] What Flathead Indians value, therefore, is an experience that is not readily fixed as an object. One would hope, though, that some sort of dialogic exchange between the two positions might be possible. For instance, I can understand musical ownership to include both the possession of music as an object and the experience of dreaming a song on the grounds that this disparity is partly generated by a mismatch between capitalist and non-capitalist notions of property. Hence, even if I cannot think entirely outside of this familiar framework, I can at least acknowledge that it is culturally constructed. Presumably, Flathead Indians also use CD players and are able to envisage more than one type and circumstance of musical ownership. Here again we encounter the problem of essentialism versus hybridity, already familiar, in relation to gender and race, from previous chapters. The solution lies in finding a way between the extreme poles of core identity and floating identity.

We have seen that entrenched partitions between Western and non-Western musics are sustained by ideologies of self and other that regard one tradition as natural and the rest as ethnic. This division prompts an array of questions: who is associated with a particular music, to whom does it belong, what is authenticity, and what is tradition? Musical ownership is highly charged because it touches on formations of nationality, ethnicity, gender, social group, peer group, and age. Music, we have learned, does not just reflect social groups, it embodies and may even define them, because people can establish identity by consolidating around a type of music. For youth culture, a strong association with a particular type of music is not just a way of forging personality, but of excluding others, especially an older generation. Here we encounter the familiar paradox that identity is enabling, but often forged through processes of expulsion.

Focusing on the second aspect, Homi Bhabha suggests we should turn around the usual literary search for the qualities of nation and ask instead what national characteristics deem to be other: what they exclude.[21] Adapting this perspective to music, we can see that styles are sometimes used to signify division. The flutes and lambeg drums of Protestant marching bands in Northern Ireland, to take an example, are rigid markers of an identity used to claim territory, to dominate urban space for a Protestant community in a way that is designed to preclude mixing with the Celtic music of the Catholic community. The music signifies a sectarian divide that is often marked by violence.[22]

Another process by which inside/outside binaries are assembled is of course the canon, which creates patterns of acceptability and difference even within traditions. The Western canon tends to value structural rigour, while banishing what might be called everyday music. Ethnomusicology's lack of allegiance to this framework implicitly criticizes a restrictive practice as one would expect from a discipline that celebrates egalitarian values. However, even though it is partly defined by its exclusion from one canon, ethnomusicology has, or did have, canons of its own, though they were defined more by shared disciplinary knowledge than by evaluative criteria. According to Bruno Nettl, the shared interests of the 1960s were: native North American music, music of sub-Saharan Africa, classical music of India, and principles of gamelan music.[23] We can understand the importance attributed to native North American music, to take one example, because scholarship in this area extends back into the nineteenth century. Continued interest stems perhaps from the available library resources, from the influence of teachers, from geographical proximity and from the status of native Americans as colonial victims.[24]

Nettl also suggests that a shared knowledge, based in Anglo-American repertoires (particularly the Child ballads) and Hungarian folk music, underpinned meetings of the International Folk Music Council in the 1950s.[25] As mentioned, folkloristics is a strand within ethnomusicology, yet the various folk traditions, within and outside Europe and North America, create disciplinary ambiguity since they do not comfortably inhabit only one space. These musics are neither inside nor outside the Western tradition, nor are they completely in step with the march of modernity: rather, they occupy the place of the other within the same geographical, if not social, space as the dominant tradition. And like non-Western musics, they are obviously linked to ethnicity and social class, in a way that the bourgeois tradition likes to pretend it is not. As we saw in Chapter 4, folk music is theorized in various ways by the bourgeois tradition; sometimes as an impoverished version of the same tradition – a diluted variant for the uneducated – sometimes as a rural practice that reinforces conceptions of town and country, and sometimes as a source of vital energy for art music. It is also studied from a sociological perspective that may be more concerned with how communities are structured than with collecting ethnographic data. In this way, it functions as a focus for the not always compatible methodologies of different disciplines.

Inside and outside perspectives are of crucial importance for ethnomusicology, which devotes much energy to overcoming the dualities between observer and observed. At an extreme, ethnomusicologists might be seen as missionary figures, trying to shoehorn other cultures into the frame of Western thought, or as imperialists imposing correct meanings on cultures, though few, if any, are likely to persevere without at least some sympathy for the tradition being studied. More ordinarily, there is a whole range of problems to be solved between the expectations of a researcher and those of the practitioners. How, for example, does the participating researcher know that what he or she experiences is the same as what the inside participants experience (a distinction between what anthropologists call etic and emic positions)? And how well do research expectations and the views of an informant align? The latter might, for example, be inclined to say what he or she thinks will please the interviewer, while the researcher's questions might obscure matters of paramount interest to the community.

Researchers are now acutely aware of these problems and try to engage in a dialogic interaction, a genuine two-way conversation that will pick up thoughts in context. Such practices understand music as embedded culture and are far removed from the rigid inside/outside binaries that characterized older classificatory schemes.[26] Many ethnomusicologists are conversant with the traditions they study to a point where inside/outside distinctions blur. They become even less distinct, of course, when the ethnomusicologist is a member of the tradition studied – in this case some estrangement from familiar surroundings may be required. In fact someone familiar with the Western tradition, attempting to study it from an anthropological angle that will challenge inbuilt perceptions of the culture, is, effectively, an insider ethnomusicologist. Somebody conversant with two traditions, moreover, will face the problems of translating between them.

A good example of the complexities of the insider/outsider dialogues is offered by Rice, who recounts his experience learning to play the *gaida* (Bulgarian bagpipes). After some lessons with a player called Kostadin Varimezov, Rice reached a degree of proficiency, but was unable to master the high ornaments that are such a distinctive part of the style. In the end, he learned to perform these through a combination of processes: he listened to recordings of Kostadin and slowed down the complex ornaments so that he could hear their components; and then, remembering comments from his teacher, experimented with fingerings. He points out that this progression was motivated by more than a desire to learn the instrument, since teacher and pupil formed a social bond that propelled the instruction towards success. Having mastered the ornaments in what, by traditional standards, would be an artificial manner, Rice was accepted as a genuine *gaida* player in the Bulgarian community. Indeed, with his knowledge of Bulgarian language, music and dances, one acquaintance suggested that he had acquired a Bulgarian identity. Thus, he had crossed over from outside observer to inside member of a living tradition, though he continued to document this experience in an academic manner. One might say that he had learned to inhabit two traditions and to translate between them. In his words, 'I speak as myself, a self formed, reconfigured, and changed by my encounters with and understandings of Bulgarian, and indeed all kinds of other, musical works and performances.'[27]

The inside/outside relationship takes place in a network of discourses affected by considerations that feed the identity of both, with gender an issue of particular importance. The scrutiny that gender studies applies to the disinterested reader is paralleled by ethnology's investigation of the ungendered researcher, recognizing that both researchers and informants may naturalize preformed gender roles in their narratives. Writing about fieldwork in village India, Carol Babiracki outlines the difference between the apparently ungendered report that formed the dissertation resulting from this work and the biographical experiences that constitute her memories of it. As a participant in village activities, she recalls that she was expected to conform to the accepted gender patterns of dances, while, as a researcher, she also tried to observe what the male dancers were doing.[28] On one occasion, however, her detached presence as the only female observing a male dance was challenged by the dancers who chose to sing to her, rejecting her posture as a disinterested observer operating a recording machine.[29]

The potential for discrepancies between the values of the researcher and those found in the researched community are huge, and play out some of the contradictions of postmodernism. These dilemmas are examined and enacted in an article by Ellen Koskoff entitled 'What Do We Want to Teach When We Teach Music?' After providing an almost normative description of a locally and pragmatically constituted postmodernism, Koskoff then expresses the wish that she might use her 'knowledge and experience of music to promote tolerance of difference – between races, ethnicities, classes, religions, sexualities and genders'. 'As an ethnomusicologist,' she continues, 'I believe in the basic tenet of our field: just as all people are inherently equal, so are their musics.'[30] This belief, despite its worthy intentions, is surely dogged by contradictions, since it universalizes diversity and would, presumably, have to respect less egalitarian viewpoints. Such paradoxes unfold when Koskoff asks how we can compare the canonic claims of equal musics when a canon is understood to be a set of works that serves to uphold and validate particular values.

One particular example she pursues involves North Indian music – specifically its capacity for preserving cultural value. Basing her account on Daniel M. Neuman's *The Life of Music in North India: The Organization of an Artistic Tradition*, she goes on to describe the determining characteristics of the *kalawant*, a hereditary vocal musician. The *kalawant*, indigenous culture stipulates, should be descended from a well-known musical ancestor, preferably with a patrilineal pedigree of at least three generations, but one which does not include *sarangi* or *tabla* players. So described, these demarcations might seem unduly severe. Yet set alongside the discriminating principles of Western canon formation, Koskoff argues, these rules are less idiosyncratic than they might at first appear. The point is certainly well made; but in asking how one might compare the regulatory precepts that underpin canon construction in different cultures, Koskoff generates other questions that she is less inclined to tackle. How, for instance, can her own beliefs about the contingency of knowledge be reconciled with traditions in which musical knowledge is considered to be far from contingent? Should she feel permitted to criticize the patrilineal privileges of the *kalawant*, or would this be to impose a Western view of rationality on another culture? Surely her dilemma is that while a broadly postmodernist critique of Western hegemony is indicative of a reflexive capacity in that same culture, in moving out of that circle she encounters a process of canon formation that is not guaranteed to be compatible with her own (universal) notions of equality.

Even without an informed view of the social practices in which North Indian music is embedded, by drawing on the information about lineage in the *kalawant* offered by Koskoff, it is possible to imagine an interface between the values it upholds and those that she espouses. Perhaps *kalawant* music can be heard stereoscopically: that is to say, its tradition and all it has done to perpetuate the music can be appreciated through one channel, while another filters out those values that would otherwise serve to exclude people from participation in this music. Such an approach would be neither inside nor outside the particular canon in question, a strategy that could also be adopted to help relieve the Western canon of its institutional arrogances without silencing its less authoritarian voices.

Turning again to Rice's discussion of Bulgarian music, we can now address some of the social configurations produced by various intersections of tradition and modernization. He describes how for this community music is a way of 'being in the world', how its symbolic forms enact identities and communities, and how the researcher's horizons are expanded by encountering a way of being in the world that music symbolically references.[31] But this world is, of course, not static, particularly under conditions of modernity. Exemplifying this condition, Rice cites the difference between the ornamental style of Kostadin and that of his nephew. Kostadin perceived his own ornaments to be authentically Bulgarian, while those of his nephew, more flashy and fashionable, were linked in his mind with Muslim Gypsy musicians. Kostadin found his own ornamentation aesthetically fulfilling because it evoked, in Rice's judgement, 'a familiar, comfortable world of previous experience, a world dominated by Bulgarians and the progress and security provided by the Communist party. His nephew's way', he continues, 'was empty aesthetically because it referenced a world of change, threat and potential instability.'[32] In this reading, Kostadin's authenticity is dependent on particular political conditions, but claims to authenticity are widespread and do not always require such specific circumstances.

As we saw in the previous chapter, authenticity in rock music is partly derived from notions of authenticity in folk music. Like the authenticity movement in classical music, the idea of community evoked by authenticity in folk is a blend of old and new: it tries to step out of modernity, without understanding that the move itself is an index of modernity. It constructs through modern ideas a vision of the past, which, in the case of Celtic music, resides not so much in a specific historical location, but in a mythic, timeless realm. Celtic music offers a way of being in the world that is occupied by a certain group of people, but can also be tapped into by others. And, of course, it is increasingly rare for any person or group of persons to be associated exclusively with one musical community: even someone who identifies predominantly with a Celtic tradition will also be exposed to more overtly commercialized musics, along with the general processes of modernity, and will therefore be accomplished at translating between traditions.

Modernization creates circumstances in which more people and musics mingle and associate. Bohlman gives as an example of this the market place, or bazaar, of a Middle Eastern city, where a huge mix of music and traditions, both old and new, live and recorded, jostle alongside one another, collapsing time and space.[33] Music associated with a particular place, this is to say, can be heard in the same space as music associated with another geographically distant location, blurring distinctions between urban and rural spaces. Such conditions affect the ways in which people learn musics, since one can acquire a particular style from a recording, as Rice demonstrates, thus accessing and potentially changing a musical identity. Indeed, notions of primary and secondary location can become confused: thus it is quite possible that the musicians participating in a traditional music session on the west coast of Ireland learned their repertoire from Frances O'Neill's publications of folk tunes and dances collected in early twentieth-century Chicago.[34] Such processes also dissolve barriers between oral and written cultures, since some aspects of a folk culture might be notated and learned in this form and then returned to an oral state. The upshot is that styles do not remain rigid, despite the efforts of those seeking authenticity, they mingle and develop. Such admixtures are the subject of Annie Proulx's novel *Accordion Crimes*, in which a button accordion stands as a metaphor for the experiences of various immigrant groups in America, as it passes from group to group, style to style.

Commodification renders the boundary between folk and pop hazy because a specific way of being in the world can be plundered to appeal to a wide audience, often turning a particular culture into a temporary fashion. Such processes can lead to exciting developments, but can also result in traditions being destroyed – in patterns of life being forced into uneasy alliances with the social patterns of modernity. Put succinctly, the ways in which musics and identities collude and collide has much to do with the space–time compression and technical innovations of modernity, which wear down established patterns of authenticity. The dark side of this procedure is that Western modernity imposes its will on those who live, in Bhabha's poignant phrase, 'otherwise than modernity'.[35] But because modernity is a reflexive process, it can also be influenced and moulded by unfamiliar experiences.[36]

I mentioned early in this section that ethnomusicology is better understood as an ethnographic method of studying music than as a musicology of non-Western music. I want to conclude the chapter by considering what musicology looks like from an ethnographic perspective. Because such an outlook is attuned to understanding music as a form of human interaction, it is most likely to examine the ways in which oral, somatic, performance-based musics are translated into textual knowledge. This is a potentially productive approach, but if pursued over-zealously can lead to rigid distinctions between text and act that are unhelpful because they rehearse binaries of precisely the type that were challenged by Derrida in his readings of Rousseau and Lévi-Strauss.[37] It is helpful to remember that notation and oral tradition are not wholly opposed poles: oral traditions rely on devices to orient participants and depend on learned patterns, while notation, at a basic stage, is merely a way of extending such devices. It is, therefore, unconvincing to perceive one as vivid and dynamic, the other as abstract and reified. The preservation of such distinctions depends on a model of authenticity that is hard to justify, since it argues that different horizons of representation are mutually exclusive.

Textual obsessions with editorial accuracy or internal procedure are undoubtedly limiting, but it would be wrong to understand them as the only approaches possible to notated music. They do not preclude more socialized readings and neither does the practice of referring to music as an object necessarily prohibit an intersubjective understanding of it as a particular configuration of subjectivity. Merriam's 'music as culture' formula is a good description of current trends that are committed to understanding music as a form of subjectivity. When Merriam's vision is applied to a wide band of musicology, it encourages us to release the human content of established modes of representation. The latter are transformed and become less rigid in the process.

6 Positions

Modernity

Postmodernism is a dominant contemporary sensibility that champions the particular over the general. With the contradiction of universal particularism at its heart, it is inherently unstable and multifaceted. Much of what has been discussed in this book – poststructuralism, gender studies, cultural studies, post-colonialism – is often categorized as postmodernist, though not all practitioners in these fields would accept the description. Postmodernism is an ensemble of discourses marked by differences of opinion and paradox, yet it also scoops up a wide range of discourses and distinguishes their activities from so-called modernist values. The postmodernist turn in musicology, for example, means that musicology has become receptive to a general body of ideas, not that it is reducible to a particular theory. This postmodernist ethos embraces both current cultural practice, which is inseparable from theoretical reflection, and the methodologies used to interpret a wider range of repertoires.

Before looking at the impact of postmodernism on musicology in general, I want to say something about modernity and modernism, postmodernity and postmodernism. Modernity and postmodernity refer to sets of social, economic and cognitive practices; modernism and postmodernism signify corresponding cultural domains. It is useful to keep these distinctions in mind, even though it is difficult not to speak of modernism in a general sense because it is such a widespread practice. Modernity is underpinned by a process of modernization and a belief in rationalization. With its drive for efficiency and faith in the new, modernization overcomes traditions and is thus both liberating and unsettling, releasing people from accepted modes of behaviour while establishing new traditions and creating uncertainties. Rationalization leads to the differentiation of distinct spheres: the technical (industrial); the economic (based on capitalist beliefs in private ownership and profit); the political (based on the legislative apparatus of the nation state); and the aesthetic (grounded in artistic autonomy). In these conditions, aesthetic modernization leads to art becoming an increasingly defined sphere with discourses of its own.

The process of modernization is dynamic, overcoming one method of manufacture or administrative organization in favour of another. The phase that we are currently experiencing is, in Western societies at least, post-industrial and marked by the rise of information technologies. In industrial and economic spheres, the mass production that enabled stable employment is replaced by consumer-led markets and mobile employment. Politically, the nation state is weakened by a localized pull towards regions and by a homogenizing pull to globalization; processes that strive simultaneously for identity and difference. Since these dynamics, despite their apparent strangeness, are better understood as intensifications of modernity than its abandonment, it makes more sense to understand postmodernity as embodying a continuation and reinterpretation of modernity than to portray it as a decisive move to a new plane of social organization. From this perspective, it is possible to understand that the transition from industrialism to information technology, for example, is underpinned by a continuing drive for efficiency. For some parts of the globe and for some sectors of society, processes of rationalization have led to increased comfort and enabled people to pursue private dreams of individual happiness. However, these attainments are offset by ecological damage and the increasing mechanization of war, while many face social exclusion and erosion of the traditions that had once anchored their beliefs.[1]

For some commentators on modernity, the rationalization accomplished by modernization is better described as rationalism, that is, as a blind belief in a limited form of cognition. Adorno's and Horkheimer's term for this is 'instrumental reason', by which they refer to an obsession with means rather than ends. This is illustrated in their *Dialectic of Enlightenment* by a reading of the sirens episode from Homer's *Odyssey*: in order to pass the sirens, Odysseus must repress himself (he orders his crew to tie him to the mast), thus the instrumental goal of navigating the ship – of forging a disciplined subjectivity – is achieved at the expense of his own desire.[2]

Extrapolating from this scenario, Adorno and Horkheimer argue that instrumental reason is accomplished by suppressing the fulfilment it is supposed to bring. A form of cognition that demands identity, that is to say, recognizes only itself in the world, is opaque to other types of experience, and cannot access the particular forms of subjectivity embedded in objects and institutions that societies have produced. Instead, it forces specific configurations of subjectivity into inappropriate moulds, damaging them in the process.

This said, it is important to understand that Adorno's critique of Enlightenment, damning as it is, is not a call for irrationality, since it condemns a domineering form of reason only and calls for a type of thinking that is more open to the distinctive qualities of objects. This point is often missed by critics of Adorno (such as Jürgen Habermas), who try to caricature his position as a retreat into contemplative aesthetics.[3] On the other hand, he is also upbraided by postmodernists for a doctrinaire modernist stance. Adorno attracts criticism from opposing modernist and postmodernist positions because he represents characteristics of both, holding together two, sometimes conflicting, strands of modernity that are often flattened into successive moments by dualistic divisions of modernism and postmodernism.

Exploring the contradictions of Western rationality is standard practice for purveyors of the postmodern message, though it is seldom done with the dialectical tension that is characteristic of Adorno. In the place of dialectical critique, Foucault offers a genealogy of power-relations that conveys the history of Western rationality as an increasingly internalized form of self-repression by which human subjects learn to regulate themselves. Emphasizing the contingency of discourses, he shows how particular types of knowledge acquire power over others by incorporating themselves into supposedly disinterested institutional practices. Unfortunately, however, he sometimes ties truth claims to power claims so closely that they become indistinguishable. Notwithstanding a sometimes one-dimensional view of modernity's control over human subjects, Foucault is significant for showing that the mechanisms for disciplining knowledge are not historically inevitable. They are, he argues, configurations that can be reworked. The prevalent idea that musicology constructs music in ways that embody dominant perceptions of gender and the body owes much to Foucault, as do subsequent attempts to construct a musicology that employs a less restrictive model of subjectivity.[4]

Derrida, we have seen, shows how the sign-unit (the semiotic equivalent of the Adornian concept) fails to achieve complete identity. For some, Derrida is heir to an Enlightenment tradition of self-critique, for others he reduces truth claims to linguistic indeterminacy.[5] This ambivalence means that deconstruction occupies a strange place in postmodernism because, while its questioning of closure remains important, its obsession with text is seen by some to be too formalist and its destabilizing tendencies considered by others to undermine valued identities. The emphasis on particularity found in feminism also leads to varying outcomes, ranging from Hélène Cixous's conflation of rationality and patriarchy, to the insistence of Toril Moi and Julia Kristeva that the critique of rationality must draw on that same tradition.[6]

From this latter perspective, extravagant critiques of bourgeois rationality, informing us that modernity and reason police the body and mind, are trapped in a conundrum because it is an already implicated logical analysis that is used to show the shortcomings of a dominant form of reason. We are now so accustomed to Foucauldian postmodernists showing modernity to be a sort of terrorism that suppresses the particular, that a history of dysfunctions obscures a capacity for reflexive transformation. However twisted perceptions of rationality may become, we are still dependent on its core potential to fight prejudice: counteracting racism and other forms of intolerance requires rational argumentation. If post-Enlightenment rationality cannot shake off a heritage of institutionalized repression, it is worth remembering that it also offers resources for combating the same deformations.

Populist brands of postmodernism tend to set up one-sided comparisons between rigid, monolithic, modernist ideology, and supple, sensitive discourses of the particular. This strategy accords the modern subject a degree of integration that it never really possessed. Had bourgeois subjectivity ever achieved the closure its detractors attribute to it, it would never have needed to buttress this ideal through aesthetic autonomy. Turning to the other side of this equation, we might enquire whether the decentred postmodern subject is really a sustainable goal. It is certainly true that a dominant tradition has prioritized a certain type of subject and marginalized others, but not all decentring of subjectivity is liberating. For one person a decentred subjectivity might signify release from stuffy customs, for another it may signify the undesired destruction of valued conventions. Identity can be a site of negotiation, defensive closure or of necessary resistance; the mix varies as it responds to different situations.

According to Jean-François Lyotard, the grand narratives of modernity seek to construct a history of progress that has become suspect and in need of replacement by more localized narratives.[7] In these circumstances representation of the world becomes increasingly linked to identity, whether rooted in gender, ethnicity, race, class or age. Previous chapters have shown, in support of this view, that generalized perceptions of knowledge do indeed serve particular interests that can be valuably challenged from a different perspective. Current critical historiography, moreover, leads us to understand that none of us could return to older kinds of history, however fragmented we might want to make them in hindsight, since they were framed by a general desire to tell synthesizing stories.

When, however, the postmodern celebration of micro-narratives reaches an extreme, it creates problems. To think that multiple narratives have replaced meta-narratives is to assume that large-scale historical processes are largely fictitious and can countenance no internal differentiation. Such a claim would have to argue, against all the evidence, that there are no discernible characteristics of global integration.[8] It would have to do so, furthermore, against clear evidence of such features in the increasingly widespread applications of standardized information technology. Of course, these properties are offset by the increasingly diverse areas of knowledge that can be accessed by the same technology. When both these tendencies are taken into account, it can be seen that standardization and diversity exist side by side without cancelling each other out, hence it is reasonable to conclude that globalization excludes neither domain.

Postmodernity itself is something of a meta-narrative when it inflates the historical conditions, not only of particular Western nations, but of a social sector within that region, to universal relevance. Consequently, we can offer postmodernity some of its own medicine and ask it to reflect on the specifics of its own historical location. Even within post-industrial Western nations there are those, whether by choice or necessity, who cling to identities more in keeping with older forms of employment, or maintain traditions that have little truck with modernity; indeed, the economic base for a large sector of eastern Europe remains industrial and modern. Outside the North Atlantic, meanwhile, there are many for whom traditional beliefs are of more importance than the discourses of modernity, let alone those of postmodernity. Of course a certain branch of ethnographic postmodernism counters such diversity to the master narratives of modernity, but there is little evidence to suggest that postmodernity has rendered the divide any less sharp. Those who live otherwise than modernity are less likely to regard new identities as vibrant, since new values may well conflict with the ways they organize their life worlds. Such people, moreover, are inclined to experience their music as a symbolic way of being in the world, rather than the depthless intensity advocated by the less culturally sensitive brands of postmodernism.[9] Even those living substantially within the institutions of modernity, or postmodernity, may struggle to find ways of reconciling traditional cultures with the anonymous steering mechanisms that order their existence.

Both embodying generalism and fighting it, postmodernism is a deeply divided condition, and its championing of diversity is as problematic as its unspoken generalism. Diversity as an end in itself would attribute to the most patriarchal and exclusive readings of music the same validity as any other. A good riposte to relativism is offered by Donna Haraway, who points out that totality and relativism are mirror images because they both propose a form of knowledge located nowhere in particular. Her alternative to this binarism is what she calls 'partial, locatable, critical knowledges sustaining the possibility of webs of connections called solidarity in politics and shared conversations in epistemology'.[10] The strength of this position is that it envisages situated knowledge, 'a view from somewhere', built on the principle that one cannot access another perspective without having one's own. 'We do not seek partiality for its own sake', she continues, 'but for the sake of connections and unexpected openings situated knowledges make possible'.[11]

Haraway's argument is valuable because it envisages affinities that extend beyond personalized interests, even if the practicalities of forming such associations are beset with difficulties. When presented subtly like this, with a commitment to problem solving, the postmodern condition becomes more appealing, since it offers prospects for overcoming some of its own limitations and, as a consequence, provides resources for transforming hardened musicology into a more flexible discipline.

Musicology and postmodernism

Before exploring how the dilemmas of postmodernism manifest themselves in musicology, it would be a good idea to revisit one of the paths that musicology took towards its present state. As we have seen, Joseph Kerman chivvied the discipline to become a critical practice, capable of participation in mainstream humanities debates. Such a perspective finds insufficient a form of historical study that blithely generates facts and, likewise, a mode of analysis that diligently pursues structural unity; instead it compels both enterprises to demonstrate their significance and to justify the artistic importance of the music at the centre of their enquiries. When perceived as constructs, both epistemologies are transformed: historical musicology becomes more aware of its own historiography and analysis becomes contextualized; both disciplines are consequently made more fluid, thereby providing resources for a transformed mode of critical enquiry. In a laudable attempt to integrate musicology with mainstream humanities research, Kerman went on to argue that it should follow the model of literary criticism. That he did so at a time when the tenets of the latter discipline were undergoing a thorough critical interrogation that even questioned the notion of a separate genre called literature is nevertheless ironic. In these circumstances, it is not surprising that his call for musicology to turn critical has been answered in some quarters (and well beyond his expectations) by a full-scale application of ideas prevalent in literary and cultural studies to musicology. It is in this vein that musicology has been able to merge with wider humanities debates, all of them set to challenge the 'common sense' view that once ruled.

Lawrence Kramer has been a pioneering figure in the reconstruction of musicology, creatively applying theoretical developments to the study of music. His most sustained statement on the matter occurs in the opening chapter to *Classical Music and Postmodern Knowledge*, 'Prospects: Postmodernism and Musicology'. Originally published as a journal article, an earlier version of this chapter appeared with a more portentous title, 'The Musicology of the Future', in which form it sparked an exchange with Gary Tomlinson that is now a musicology classic.[12] Claiming that the 'conceptual and rhetorical world of postmodernism' offers the best resources for a musicology rooted in human interest, Kramer describes his brand of postmodernism as 'not a system but an ethos', an ethos with strategies, following Haraway's lead, that are 'localized, heterogeneous, contestatory, and contested'.[13] He is well aware that postmodernism is often taken to mean many different things and is susceptible to a certain modishness, while noting that 'without some appeal to standards of truth and falsehood, reality and illusion, reason and unreason, neither social institutions nor consensus belief can competently be criticized'.[14] Furthermore, he acknowledges that postmodernism is dependent on modernism and not wholly oppositional to it,[15] but this point is somewhat obscured by his enthusiasm for a new conceptual and rhetorical milieu, which, in a language seemingly with a will of its own, is quick to condemn modernism.

Despite this tendency, what he describes as a postmodernist reading is in many ways a reawakening of strands already present in modernism. In this sense, his project is more a rereading of modernism than a rejection of it, though the performative effect of his writing is to emphasize the gap between modernism and postmodernism more than their connection or transformation. This diagnosis is both confirmed and skewed by the exchange with Tomlinson, triggered by Kramer's hopes for a postmodernist musicology. Both authors consider themselves to be postmodernist, but cannot agree on what they mean by this, nor on how postmodernism breaks with modernism. On the one hand, both writers agree, tacitly, that to be left holding the card marked 'modernist' would be an embarrassment: when Kramer is accused of favouring categories 'darkly tinted for us with modernist ideology', it is the accusation rather than the diagnosis of something insidiously menacing that he choses to rebut.[16] On the other hand, the latter's impressive defence amounts to a sustained critique of postmodernist paradoxes, questioning in particular how unknowable subject positions can ever begin to communicate with one another. In a sense, Tomlinson is correct to suppose that Kramer harbours certain modernist tendencies. Yet, to my mind, it is these inclinations, even in the course of transformation, that imbue his discourse with a necessary critical edge. By contrast, although the desire to understand music as a worldly activity is commendable, Tomlinson's demonizing of modernism is altogether less helpful because it threatens to homogenize a highly differentiated cultural phenomenon and thereby obscure the perception of alterity that he seeks.

Tomlinson's favoured methodology of thick reading finds resemblances between Gadamer's historical hermeneutics, Foucault's genealogy and post-colonial theory.[17] He locates in these methodologies a willingness to experience the potential strangeness of the 'others' we encounter through music, applying an ethnographic approach that echoes the dilemmas raised by ethnomusicology. He tackles Western music, mainly of the Renaissance, with a view to estranging accepted models of it and finding subdued voices. Speaking of Kramer's reading of Mozart's String Trio K. 563, he asks: 'where has *Mozart* gone – Mozart, a mysterious and elusive subjectivity whom . . . we too easily come to believe we know well?'[18] Tomlinson's desire to encounter an unknown Mozart embodies, he argues, a 'contextualism that will not circle back narrowly to the notes but instead will *resolutely historicize musical utterance*, exploding it outwards through an imaginative building of contexts out of as wealthy a concatenation of past traces as the historian can manage'.[19] Hoping to avoid categories such as 'work', 'art', 'text', and emphasizing the locality of knowledge, he seeks encounters with the historical subjectivities that texts embody in particular formations.

This aim (which has affinities with cultural studies' search for the social life of subjective forms) is radical because it involves dissolving what is normally understood to be music into unfamiliar historical voices. For all its interest, however, it obscures the irreducibly specific dimension of music: its particularity as sound.[20] For while it is true that the apparent inscrutability of sound can be used to block cultural reading, a case can also be made in support of cultural history extending its reach to include sonic textures. Moreover, Tomlinson is somewhat overwhelmed by spectres of the knowledge-seeking subject as a sort of terrorist that subjugates others.[21] In trying to escape from this vision, he raises the prospect of somehow escaping one's own subjectivity and finding something else. Whatever the allure of this aspiration, Kramer adds a necessary corrective when he argues that it is not necessary to depreciate one's own subjectivity in order to appreciate someone else's. Instead, it is necessary to understand how one's own subjectivity is constituted – when this happens, subjectivity becomes less defensive and functions more like what Kramer calls a 'position in a continuous process of communicative exchange'.[22]

Both Kramer and Tomlinson acknowledge the influence of the new historicism, with its commitment to thick description, on their approaches. Mainly encountered in literary studies, this is not an easy movement to describe since those who are normally considered to be its exponents deny that it is a programmatic critical movement. Arram Veeser, however, manages to identify five points that new historicists agree on, two of which have particular relevance here. Firstly, 'that every expressive act is embedded in a network of material practices';

and, secondly, 'that literary and non-literary "texts" circulate inseparably'.[23] The second point requires modification to apply to music, since a Freudian case study, say, can be read as literary text, but not obviously as music. In order to find parallels, if any, between the two, one needs to understand them both as embodying social actions: both as embedded, as the first point suggests, in a network of social practices. In this vein, Kramer takes from the new historicism what he calls the following cornerstone principle: 'music, as a cultural activity, must be acknowledged to help produce the discourses and representations of which it is also the product'.[24] A further characterization of new historicist readings is that they will often address a text from a historical perspective that is considered to be marginal from a traditional historical viewpoint, or will unfold a thick context from an unlikely source. We have already seen in Chapter 3 an example of such an approach in Richard Leppert's discussions of the bourgeois attitudes embodied in depictions of music in paintings. Through such art, he is able to address issues such as constructions of gender, the relationships between public and private space, and representations of colonial power.[25]

Historicist themes are also at work when Kramer discusses the dialogue of consumption and the exotic in Ravel's *Daphnis and Chloé* (as seen in Chapter 5), though his reading is a far from dogmatic display of methodology. It is, presumably, an example of the post-modernist musicology that the following manifesto advocates:

> It should be possible to recast musicology as the rigorous and contestable study, theory, and practice of musical subjectivities. This would be a musicology in which the results of archival and analytical work, formerly prized in their own right, would become significant only in relation to subjective values – which is not to say the values of an atomised private inwardness, but those of a historically situated type of human agency. Such a musicology would satisfy the demand for human interest, not by making good on music's lack of meaning, but by ceasing to entertain the illusion that such a lack ever existed.[26]

This statement provides a good summary of current aspirations and offers tantalizing prospects for the future. Yet its pluralist outlook has, ironically, something of a programmatic feel to it – as if musicology will eventually become a certain type of activity or, at least, as if one strand will assume the highest merit. Granted, all musicology deals with subjectivity, but in an ensemble of discourses not all components need be concerned directly with the same aspect. Analysis, for example, when rid of formalist fundamentals, describes and generates musical structures that are indeed socially mediated. However, surely these need not always be decoded precisely because the behaviour of social codes transposed into another medium (music) is interesting in itself. Nevertheless, we can no longer pretend that music is not a social practice, nor that it is immune from wide-ranging cultural debates. Kramer's willingness to find new latencies in the classical repertoire, to release it from the ligature of its own institutions and discourses, is of great significance for an age that no longer takes the value of such music for granted.

Culture

Moving away from formulations of postmodernism as an interpretive ethos, I shall now turn to postmodernist culture, initially taking an Adornian glance at how music engages with modernity. Much of the modernist impulse in music can be traced back to Beethoven and his reception history. In Beethoven we find the temporal dynamic of modernity harnessed to a search for new forms of material expression. His middle period, in particular, offers a model of the integrated bourgeois subject that could be only an ideal in everyday life. But at the same time the specificity and sensuality of Beethoven's music also alerts the same subject to what its need for totality excludes. This dialectic takes on a different hue when Wagner, adding drama to the mix, tries to mythologize a grandiose bourgeois subjectivity, because the illusion of seamless cohesion becomes fissured by its own excess.

Post-Wagnerian music, what might be called modernism proper, pursues the goal of inventing new material in a self-conscious manner and is beholden to an aesthetic of the new, even – as in Stravinsky's case – when avoiding a post-Wagnerian sound. However, this innovation takes place in a particular cultural milieu that was underestimated as subsequent modernist aesthetics came to value the inventions of early twentieth-century innovators such as Stravinsky and Schoenberg over the cultural context of the nineteenth-century residue from which this music emerged. Consequently, the task of reawakening that environment has fallen to recent musicology.

The striving for innovation hardened after the Second World War into the high-modernist, structuralist aesthetic pioneered by composers such as Pierre Boulez in Europe and Milton Babbitt in the United States. Based at Princeton University, Babbitt specifically compared compositional innovation to scientific research, and allowed the goal of structural integration to marginalize the signifying codes through which music operates.[27] In doing so, he espoused core modernist beliefs that translated into the analytical methodologies (notably set theory) that followed his lead. Boulez, meanwhile, had been outspoken since the 1950s about the museological culture that dominated the performance, reception and recording of classical music and thereby stifled developments in new music. His solution in the mid-1970s was to found IRCAM (Institut de Recherche et Coordination Acoustique/Musique), a music research institute situated adjacent to the Centre Georges Pompidou in central Paris. Dedicated to the intersection of music and technology, IRCAM is based on the model of a scientific research institute in which specialists pool their expertise, with particular attention paid to the interaction of acoustic instruments with live electronics. IRCAM stands for the insitutionalization of modernist values, but has also pushed these a long way beyond the narrow concerns of the 1950s.[28]

One of the contradictions of constructivist composition Boulez has responded to in his work at IRCAM is the tendency for system-based scores, such as his *Structures*, for two pianos, to create significant discrepancies between the way we hear the score and the way it has been assembled.[29] Aware that dense construction produces indeterminacy, John Cage (who shared many of Boulez's preoccupations in the 1950s) made a virtue of the fact and turned it into a compositional technique. His *Music of Changes*, a cycle of piano pieces, is based, like a serial score, on predetermined materials and rules, but the arrangement and sequence of events was decided by tossing coins. The result is a very detailed score containing determinate events arrived at by indeterminate means. Later pieces such as *Variations IV* project indeterminacy into the performance by allowing the performers to assemble their own score from a set of instructions.

Such responses to indeterminacy are symptomatic of the transition between structuralism and poststructuralism (itself a manifestation of the broader passage from modernism to postmodernism), in which controlling structure becomes increasingly contingent. The anonymous mechanisms used by both serialist and indeterminate methods of composition share a willingness to place listener and composer alike at the mercy of abstract codes. This experience may be alienating, but it frees the listener to construct textual meanings from the event, a prospect that Cage facilitated, but was a by-product of his emphasis on the sounds themselves. Theory, of course, teaches us that we do not need to wait for such permissions before we choose our listening stategies. Moreover, Cage's eagerness to subject classical music to chance procedures in his *Europeras*, to take an example, appears less radical in an age when the canon exerts a weakened grip.

The most obvious feature of the musics that broke away from high modernist orthodoxy is the hugely expanded range of materials and styles on which they draw. This relaxation is immediately apparent in American minimalism, associated with composers such as Steve Reich and Philip Glass, which retains an interest in processes, but applies them to, what is for many, a reassuring tonal idiom. Building on this foundation, the post-minimalist composer Michael Torke has created an eclectic style that seeks to combine the raw energy of rock with the precision of chamber music. Meanwhile, other American composers, such as Robert Rochberg, have found refuge in the classical tradition, drawing on Beethoven and Mahler as emotional resources. Tonal references can also be found in the very different sound world of German composer Wolfgang Rihm, where they contribute to a style that draws on various influences, including modernist idioms, and derives much of its substance from negotiating between them.[30]

If modernism can be employed as a specific style, a musicologist might conclude from Rihm's music, then we can examine its historical location and are not compelled to experience it as an overbearing presence. Because postmodernism encourages us to reread modernism, looking at it contextually instead of purely structurally, the perceived divide between (modernist) abstraction and (post-modernist) contextualism is reduced. The difference becomes instead one between a material that relies on intrinsic relationships and a medium that mixes internal and external codes. But since all musical material is socialized, the gap is not huge: in one case, social functions are disguised; in the other, as music becomes semantically broader and willing to look beyond its own internal configurations, the associations of various components become part of a signifying network.[31]

These aesthetic transformations are mirrored across a range of cultural practices, of which none has been discussed in greater detail than architecture, probably because style is of great public interest in this sphere. The two dominant voices in this field are Robert Venturi and Charles Jencks, who criticize modernist architecture not just for its utilitarian bleakness, but for its lack of communication. Modernism, they argue, fails to understand that form, colour and texture engage their surroundings in dialogue. Buildings, they suggest, acquire meanings not just from their intrinsic properties, but from the ways in which they are viewed and from the life processes that take place within and around them. This perspective is intended to support a move from modernism to postmodernism, but (as the above discussion of music would lead us to expect) it also partly blurs the two because a contextualized reading of modernist architecture expands the semantic space within which it operates.

Jencks's preference is for architecture that consciously engages its methods of signification, thereby adapting to varying environments. The results are inclusive and diverse, whether within a single building or across a range of buildings, but fall into two main categories. Firstly, established styles can be pastiched, in which case a new building becomes almost indistinguishable from the style it copies – Quinlan Terry's Georgian Terraces in Richmond, London, fall into this category. Secondly, a building can interpret its vicinity in a more eclectic manner, as demonstated by James Stirling's and Michael Wilford's 'Clore Gallery' addition to the Tate Gallery, London (1982–86). Abutting different materials and styles, it continues the cornice line from the classical gallery and borrows the red and white theme of adjacent brickwork, while the main entrance of this 'garden building' uses green mullioned glass and the more functional rear draws on late modernist style.[32]

Such dialogues are taken further in installation art, which is not burdened with the practical responsibilities of architecture. Hovering between the two realms, Rachel Whiteread's celebrated concrete cast of a terraced house marked for demolition in Hackney, London, solidifies, in an estranged density that turns space into form, the lives that were once enacted in a now abandoned community.[33] Elsewhere within the field of visual art, the embargo that abstraction placed on figurative art has crumbled under pressure from critical discourses that challenge accepted conventions of representation, thereby enhancing the semantic sphere in which art operates and enabling fluid dialogues between different fields of signification.

Tilting the codes that construct images has been a constant theme in the work of the American Cindy Sherman, whose photographic images often reference the world of mass culture. Speaking of the made-up young woman and her mirrored face in *Untitled Film Still #2* (1977), Hal Foster comments: 'Sherman captures the gap between imagined and actual body images that yawns in each of us, the (mis)recognition where fashion and entertainment industries operate every day and night.'[34] By relentlessly drawing attention to the mechanisms that signify in her images, Sherman challenges us to encounter the codes that fashion our lives. Her dialogues between art and mass cultures play on the blurring of the high/low divide that has been such a feature of postmodernist culture, evinced by the institutionalization of pop and near complete acceptance of consumer culture. With the demolition of rock's (modernist) claims to resist mass culture, pop could celebrate its commodity status, epitomizing Fredric Jameson's claim that 'postmodernism is the consumption of sheer commodification as process'.[35] We noted earlier that this process is embodied in Madonna's music-videos, which present various identities as commodities to be consumed, as lifestyle choices (offering as choice what Sherman displays as a gap between image and industry). And it is not just popular music that flaunts its commodity status: under conditions of globalization, all sorts of traditions can be harnessed to the ubiquitous world beat.

Classical music is not immune from these circumstances, though it occasionally puts up a fight. The prestige of the classical canon can no longer be taken for granted, and its status lives on in an afterlife that signifies 'posh' or 'heritage' in the language of advertising and film. Like cuisine or interior design, classical music provides lifestyle choices, tapping into a leisure industry that enables consumers to purchase identities and images – to occupy certain social spaces.[36] Analysing a Citroen car commercial, Nicholas Cook shows how the overture to Mozart's *The Marriage of Figaro* is utilized for its proximity to classical aesthetics and for its energy, evoking images of both beauty and lively precision in a concoction that attempts to fuse nature and technology in the image of car.[37] The eponymous hero of the British TV detective series *Inspector Morse*, meanwhile, drives a vintage Jaguar around meandering lanes in Oxford, and seeks solace from the banality of police work by drinking real ale and listening to nineteenth-century opera, reserving particular enthusiasm for soprano arias. In this configuration, classical music signifies an old-world charm, a set of values that can only just hold its own in the administered world, though Morse's erudition does manage to cut through dreary procedure. Elsewhere, one only has to look at CD covers to see classical performers borrowing the images of magazine culture. The transcendentalist corporatism of Herbert von Karajan (his hands and face emerge from blackness on the LP cover of a Berlin

Philharmonic recording of Strauss's *Ein Heldenleben*)[38] is replaced by the easy-going, friendly conductor; a transformation that goes all the way to the post-punk persona of violinist Nigel Kennedy.

The combination of market pressures and internal contradictions in the discourses of classical music are played out in the authentic performance movement (we have already encountered some of its paradoxes in Chapter 2) in which the dynamics of the modernism/postmodernism debate are clearly evident. The project operates on two fronts: one extends the canon into the potential strangeness of the past and attempts to find performance styles for new (that is, very old) musics; the other reappraises the traditional repertoire and its established performance conventions. On the second front, authentic performance is what might be called the punk rock of classical music, eschewing the homogenous, thick sounds of the Berlin Philharmonic for the accident-prone interjections of valveless horns and squawking woodwind. If the search for authenticity is a quest for an origin of the type deconstruction loves to lay hands on, it can also be understood in less austere terms as an attempt to disperse a smooth orchestral sound so as to create a varied timbral range, more in keeping with the dappled surface of a postmodernist milieu.

The search for authenticity allows us to be influenced by less familiar identities, and enables us to learn, for example, how modulations are enhanced by the fizzy sound of stopped horns. Nevertheless, it is a modern performance that is created,[39] and this shaping reinforces the, by now familiar, point that one cannot shed one's own subjectivity and encounter something utterly other, since the past is always accessed from a particular location, even though the dialogic exchange may cause that location to move. Because authenticity is a mix of invention and replication, the two can easily become muddled. Roger Norrington's recording of Beethoven's Ninth Symphony demonstrates this point through a certain confusion about authorial intention that both buttresses and undermines the composer's status. By following Beethoven's metronome markings, he honours the text and composer, but simultaneously attempts to remove Beethoven from the aesthetic of transcendentalism and heroic gravitas upon which such authority depends. It is as if Beethoven's supremacy is used to dissolve the reception history that did so much to establish it in the first place. In conclusion, the net result of authentic performance, however ambigious its claims, is that the varied sonorities of original instruments are used to reinterpret the canon for a contemporary downsized aesthetic. The aftermath is that musicians are now more attuned to differing performance styles, hence the canon and its extended family start to look like various identities. And that, of course, is how postmodernist musicology hears the vast array of music at its disposal.

Framing the Fifth

Many of the issues contested between older and newer practices of musicology relate to canon formation. By managing a canonic heritage, traditional musicology upholds beliefs and values that once seemed natural and uncontroversial. However, recent musicology, following debates in other humanities disciplines, has sought to show that the canon is a social and even ideological construct. This observation is of mixed benefit since its potential to rearrange rigid beliefs about the canon is offset by a capacity to accelerate an already dwindling public interest in classical music. Occupying a privileged place in the canon, Beethoven's Fifth Symphony provides an ideal platform from which to examine this disputed territory. For good measure the symphony's reception history is one of structural integration, depth, grand narrative, teleology and utopianism, along with a few other shockers.

So how does this canonizing process take place? Largely through a reception history that has prized values found in Beethoven's heroic style and tried to universalize them. It is well known that biographical information about Beethoven links the Fifth with heroic struggle. For E.T.A. Hoffmann, meanwhile, the symphony evokes the essence of romanticism, perceived as 'the realm of the colossal and immeasurable', and simultaneously confirms the superiority of instrumental music.[40] Wagner, who could hardly support Hoffmann's views on instrumental music, also hears something monumental;[41] indeed the music came to embody the Kantian sublime, which the philosopher had only envisaged originally in relation to nature. Even Hanslick and Schenker acknowledge that the music embodies struggle; even Hanslick's doctrine of formalism makes space for views that are about far more than the music itself, as demonstrated when he comments that Brahms's Third Symphony has a 'heroic' element, 'with musical characteristics that recall the healthy soundness of Beethoven's middle period'.[42] It is well known that Schenker also resorts to metaphors about musical material, in his case natural and theological – which have invited deconstruction – to support his preference for an Austro-German canon,[43] in which the Fifth with its rigorous construction occupies dead centre. Both theorists are partial to a particular type of material, but listen covertly for a specific type of subjectivity – one that provides the illusion of autonomy and self-determination, one, that is to say, in which sensuous impulses are contained by the formal whole.

The sorts of assumptions that underlie traditional attitudes towards the canon are also evident in the descriptive analyses of Donald Tovey, which attempt to reveal the eternal verities propounded by the great man behind the music. When theorized, however, Tovey's deep truths emerge as representations of a particular subjectivity, rather than embodiments of universal values. Consider his comments on the Andante of the Fifth Symphony: 'The andante I have left without illustration. Shakespeare's women have the same courage, the same beauty of goodness, and the same humour.'[44] Apart from making a massive generalization about the characteristics displayed by Shakespeare's female characters, this remark suggests that the subjectivity of the Fifth will be understood by those of a certain noble persuasion, without considering how this conviction is assembled. In other words, it simply plugs interpretation into a certain image of femininity. Tovey's problem is not that he links music to subjectivity, but that he fails to understand the framing of his model. However, the limitations of his outlook need not be a reason to devalue Beethoven's Fifth Symphony, nor the canon in general. When pursued dialectically, theory is fully capable of drawing attention to the enlightened aspects of bourgeois subjectivity alongside its limitations.

Scott Burnham suggests recouping Beethoven by distinguishing between what he calls Beethoven's hero and Beethoven Hero.[45] The former is the heroic impulse that undoubtedly informs the Fifth Symphony, the latter the way that idea, in a heroic image of Beethoven himself, is translated into analytical norms. Beethoven's heroic style is essential to the methodologies advanced by Schenker, Burnham argues, but because, unlike A.B. Marx, he conceals this outlook, the heroic style becomes congealed in the idea of the closed, unified work that becomes a norm for music, and against which other music is judged. As a canonic figure, then, Beethoven is used as a yardstick, so opposition to this standard also tends to equate his music with a certain authority. This process, as described by Burnham, has certainly occurred, but it is difficult to make a clean break between the music and its institutionalization, since the heroic style is dependent on discourses that are as much part of the music as the entrance of the trombones in the Finale. Closure and strength cannot be expunged, but they can be rethought and so can analytical strategies that promote them. When Schenkerian theory is released from nineteenth-century organicist concepts and their twentieth-century formalist counterpart, voice-leading ceases to be an instrument of rigid orthodoxy. We can then understand more easily that Schenkerian methodology is attuned to certain types of process in certain categories of construction.

The problem boils down, then, to how convincing the Fifth and its reception history remain as models of subjectivity. It has to be admitted that the self-determining, autonomous subject associated with this symphony is not a wholly convincing projection for an era sensitive to the intersubjective formation of even our inner lives. Its synthesis is over-determined for an environment in which the negotiation of subjectivities and musical forms is as attuned to difference as to integration. Experienced as a historical meta-subject, Beethoven's model creates another problem because after the twentieth century we are unlikely to be convinced that history surges forward in a blaze of C major. Nevertheless, whatever our misgivings about these formations of modernity, we are still not free of them. To believe that we live in a post-historical age or to think that local histories have supplanted global forces is to ignore the evidence before us. The Fifth possesses the dynamic properties of classical modernity: it refashions resources to create new materials, and this process is still recognizable, if transformed, in the cultural production of a global economy, though we may feel less ebullient about it. Alongside its integrative accomplishments, the Fifth also opens form to what would be excluded by instrumental reason, namely, the particularities much loved by postmodernism. In this way the music partly demystifies the canonic ideology it is sometimes deemed to uphold. This point is lost on those strands of postmodernism that can only find images of totality in bourgeois subjectivity, and which correspondingly assume that culture simply maps onto the prevailing rationality of its day.

Locating a moment in which the symphony affords some respite from the motivic rigours of the first movement, namely the oboe cadenza in the recapitulation (bar 268), Kramer notes that the symphony incorporates what he calls 'problematical encounters with the feminine'.[46] Experienced somatically, the primary impulse of the symphony suggests a body hammered and disciplined into shape, and its model of struggle and resolution conforms to what is sometimes considered to be the masculine qualities of classical narrative. Against this background, the cadenza does indeed turn the prevailing mood to more sensory impulses.[47] But the situation is complex because gendering the logic of the music tends to repeat, with a reversed spin, the standard archetypes about masculine activity versus feminine passivity. The problem with implying that the conceptual organization of the Fifth is a predominantly masculine affair is that it effectively deprives the feminine of a powerful, logical apparatus. The interplay of the particular with the larger form is too multidimensional to be captured entirely by gendered or somatic codes. The sheer energy of the Fifth defies complete conceptual closure.

Even the most triumphalist moment in the symphony, the eruption of the Finale, is thematized by the emergence from darkness to light, rather than simply promoted. As Kramer observes, it is C minor that wins in the coda of the first movement, while C major erupts without transition in the Andante. Together these strategies prepare and heighten the transition to the C major Finale – achieved as much through intensity and liminality as by structural coherence.[48] Furthermore, this process is repeated in the approach to the recapitulation, by means of the celebrated return of the Scherzo in the Finale (bar 153). Formally, the Scherzo's restitution acts as a slackening that accentuates the splendour of the returning opening theme through contrast, while transforming the stable dominant into a less stable dominant seventh.

Pursuing this idea further, Burnham clusters a number of poetic readings around Tovey's suggestion that the Scherzo returns as a memory, referring in particular to Hermann Kretzschmar's spectral hearing of the visitation and to E.M. Forster's famous description both of the transition to the Finale and the retransition to the triumphant apotheosis of the symphony.[49] Finally, adding his own perspective, the narrating voice of memory, Burnham suggests, is the solo oboe that occurs at key points in the symphony, including the present passage (bar 172; see Ex. 4) and the previously mentioned moment in the recapitulation of the first movement. In Forster's *Howard's End*, the character Helen hears in the Scherzo goblins that signify panic and emptiness; emotions that are scattered by the heroic blasts of the Finale, only to return before the final surge. As the novel puts it: 'amid vast roarings of superhuman joy, he led his Fifth Symphony to its

Ex. 4

♩. = 96
172
1.
Hb.
p
Kl.
Hrn
(C)
pizz.
Vl.
pizz.
pizz.
arco
Br.
pizz.
Vc.
180
Hb.
Kl.
Hrn
(C)
pp
pp
Vl.
Vla
Vc.

conclusion. But the goblins were there. They could return. He said so bravely, and that is why one can trust Beethoven when he says other things.'[50] Forster's upshot is that because Beethoven is honest in his readiness not to expel doubt at the moment of apotheosis, the music acquires a moral force. And it is this integrity that inspires Burnham to conclude that 'the Beethovenian sonata form becomes a voice of human significance, telling the grand themes of quest, renewal, and closure'.[51]

His point is valid, but does the collection of readings he has assembled, which speak variously of emptiness, dread, absence, ghosts and the supernatural, not suggest that these grand themes are a little more troublesome than his affirmation would indicate? If, as Kretzschmar proposes, the return of the Scherzo is like the ghost of Banquo appearing at Macbeth's feast table, then an absence is located at the heart of an overwhelming presence; if Forster's goblins convey emptiness and dread, something unworldly, then the apotheosis is likewise spooked. Taken together, these readings identify a hollowed subject that cannot completely match its own ideals, and which is consequently less amenable to social harmony than might be thought. That is to say, if Beethoven depicts a divided subject, even amidst vast roarings of superhuman joy, the superabundant ebullience is stalked by something it cannot subdue: the abandon and confidence of the Finale harbours something other. Furthermore, this logic of dependence is tied to problem of iterability since the splendour of the opening to the Finale cannot be easily repeated without dissipating its uniqueness; indeed it is almost a critical commonplace post-Tovey to say that the liminality of the Scherzo transition and its return (themselves dependent on a future plenitude) is what offsets the grand certainty of the main theme. In short, even though the passage to the recapitulation is harmonically unproblematic, it implants a ghostly absence on which the triumpant presence of the recapitulation relies.

Does Beethoven exorcise this spectral other, we might ask? If we believe Forster's narrative, then he does not. He overwhelms it but does not expel it: he lives with it and its emptiness haunts the moment of triumph, imbuing the music with a moral force. The moment of synthesis, this is to say, is dependent on something other than itself, something that a broad swathe of reception history identifies as spectral. The other as a revenant is a theme that finds a corollary in Derrida's spectral readings of Karl Marx, whereby he seeks to locate deconstruction within the critical legacy of modernity by showing that there are more spirits of Marx than the totalizing one that is normally used to represent him.[52] Understood in this sense, a 'spectropoetic' reading of the Fifth, to use Derrida's terminology, does not unravel the symphony's syntax and reveal its real message to be one of despair and negation. It suggests, rather, that because Beethoven's grand themes are more contingent than is sometimes supposed, narrative closure is not the only spirit of the Fifth. Furthermore, one might add, if there is more than one legacy of Beethoven, it is reasonable to believe domination is not the only legacy of modernity.

It is true that the canonic view of the Fifth serves to uphold a rigid model of bourgeois subjectivity. Nevertheless, when the music is released from such a constraint, it functions as the embodiment of a negotiated subjectivity rather than a model for what subjectivity should be; thus the heroic element survives, but in a less inflated form. Heard from this position, the force-field of the Fifth becomes less an object to subdue us and more a text with which to interact. The mode of overcoming that is inherent in the heroic subject becomes, in these conditions, an incentive to overcome the dominant image of Beethoven.[53] In the possibility of struggle and overcoming, of transformation of self and circumstances, there is a message of wide human interest. What it will mean to people depends on the ways in which the tradition that influences reception of the Fifth intersects with the cultural environments of its listeners. They will certainly be able to draw on its energy, which derives as much from particular moments, from immersion in the sound, as from structural articulation; and nowhere more so than in the transition to the Finale. Such moments loosen identity and consequently slacken established modes of behaviour, enabling one to at least contemplate reconfiguring the mechanisms that control everyday life.

The current tendency to view utopian thought as a search for purity that serves to expunge anything deemed different or undesirable from an absolute ideal forgets that it is also an agent of change. Utopian thought need not be absolute: the transformation of a particular situation, rather than its supersession, might be utopian; so might an affinity established between previously incompatible positions. Nor need the nineteenth-century reception history that associates the Fifth with the sublime automatically reinforce a history of closure, since the Kantian sublime encourages us to think beyond accepted conceptual limits and even envisages a loss of self. If, despite all this, the strongest images of the heroic style contain a streak that is too domineering, it is as well to remember that this is not all Beethoven has to offer. The monumental style of the first movement of the *Appassionata* sonata is offset by the liquidity of its finale, while the Sixth Symphony offers a very different model of subjectivity than its predecessor. Both are life-enhancing.

Situating Beethoven in a wide cultural arena need not, as many cultural theorists assume, diminish the Fifth. To think so shows an unwitting subservience to the notion of the canon as a collection of totally autonomous masterpieces, and suggests that stripped of its armour plating the canon is a chimera. It is as if when we discover that the canon is not everything we were told that it suddenly becomes an insidious hoax. This view is represented by the most extreme manifestations of cultural studies, which rightly point out that all culture is a construction, but wrongly deduce from this premiss that value is simply a matter of relative taste. This attitude fails to distinguish between the specificity of certain codes and can undermine the capacity for sheer imagination and creativity to alter aesthetic experience. While it is true that both TV commercials and the Fifth manipulate codes, this information does not render the two automatically interchangeable as cultural entities. The former frequently uses conventional codes to convey established meanings, whatever the skill involved, while the latter produces a rich mix, and does so with a level of insight and brilliance that makes it an astonishing achievement. Given Beethoven's ability to turn tonality towards the prevalent models of world understanding of his day, to situate and to embody the subject, it is not surprising that the Fifth is valued. We are not, as often suggested, faced with a choice between a staunch defence of bourgeois values,[54] or an equally staunch dismissal of bourgeois ideology. The alternative position retains the transformative energy of the bourgeois tradition, while unfettering a closed and exclusive subjectivity.

Musicology now acknowledges that the ways in which music is institutionally framed and categorized are intrinsic to our interpretive attitudes, it seeks to examine and renegotiate the processes by which such dispositions crystallize, and it attempts to debate the contested attitudes, assumptions and desires that inform musical discourses. Having once rejected the descriptive excesses of Hoffmann and Wagner, in favour of an apparent objectivity, musicology is now willing to revisit this language and to examine its underlying attitudes. This approach will challenge the canon's claim to be the defining condition of music, but the disintegration of rigid beliefs is likely to be offset by enriched experiences of familiar music. A symphony about struggle will surely provide resources to liberate us from encrusted dogma.

Reconstructing musicology

My theme is that musicology, like other humanities disciplines, is faced with the ticklish task of reconstructing the humanist tradition from which it sprang. Much has been learned from deconstructing this legacy, but musicology should consider making best use of the remains and moving on. Somewhere between the certainties of conventions and contemporary pressures to become part of a lifestyles industry lies the future of musicology. The challenge is to navigate between rigid authenticities and the pressure to reduce music to packages of identity.

Of course, musicology is now influenced by an array of discourses that hark from further afield than the humanities, and confusion often arises when methodologies work at cross-purposes. Debates frequently ensue when the findings of one discipline are interpreted according to the criteria of another. We can imagine, for example, that a sociological study of an urban musical community would examine its economic status, while an ethnographic investigation might ask how its culture is represented. A music analyst, meanwhile, may look for defining musical characteristics in a specific song. Musicology clearly needs to understand that particular methodologies are geared to extracting certain information, and should be judged appropriately. But the situation is seldom this simple when the goal is a multidimensional understanding of music. Such contextual comprehension requires interdisciplinary work that not only translates across disciplines, but blurs their boundaries. Such blurring is of course part of the postmodern world, with all its dilemmas and paradoxes, that musicology inhabits.

We have seen that some forms of postmodernism, despite a general suspicion of grand narrative, universalize a set of conditions found in developed Western economies and apply them to societies that either occupy more traditional forms of modernity, or live otherwise than modernity. Such postures are prone to prejudge because they unwittingly generalize a particular set of conditions, while condemning the grand narratives of modernity. They need to become more differentiated, to examine their own historical-geographical location, and to recognize greater diversity within the conditions of modernity. The project of modernity is exploitative and homogenizing, but it is also reflexive and able to modify its own procedures.

Musicology has much to gain from understanding how these dynamics affect its own enquiries, and benefits likewise from an ability to reflect on its own conventions and locations. Musicology, like music, possesses persuasive powers; and these performative strategies need to be analysed to see how a particular approach pushes towards certain conclusions. This is a way of saying that musicology should be theoretically informed, that it cannot stand aside from its own strategies. We have seen in the course of this book that one of the most delicate problems of modern theory is played out in musicology: namely, how to show that subject positions are constructed without simply relativizing them. Since it can only speak from a constructed subject position, musicology needs to show both how it is situated by, and how it shapes, music. Approached like this, the canon need not be caricatured by its most rigid positions, since these can often be modified to understand the music in a different discursive landscape.

Theoretically informed musicology is democratic because it finds ways of translating across disciplines and rendering elitist institutions more egalitarian. Understanding how discourses function, and considering the interests they serve, greatly enhances the transparency of communication. Enhanced interaction, in its turn, increases the chances of mutual comprehension between differing outlooks and experiences. Capable of nudging sensibilities in new directions, musicology is a fully socialized medium that participates in the construction and negotiation of identity. Like music, musicology does not just reflect what happens elsewhere; it offers ways of inhabiting and shaping the world.

Notes

Notes to Preface

1. Culler makes a similar point in *Literary Theory*, 4.

2. For a critique of such oppositions, see Eagleton, *The Illusions of Postmodernism*.

3. For an expansive understanding of musical modernity, see Chua, *Absolute Music*.

Notes to Chapter 1

1. Useful discussions of Adler, to which the current exposition is indebted, can be found in Samson, 'Analysis in Context' and in Nettl, 'The Institutionalization of Musicology'.

2. For more on Seeger, see Kerman's *Musicology*.

3. Dahlhaus, *Nineteenth-Century Music*, 8–15.

4. Kerman, *Musicology*, 75.

5. For discussion along these lines, see Treitler, 'The Power of Positivist Thinking', a review of Kerman's *Musicology*.

6. Taruskin, 'The Pastness of the Present and the Presence of the Past', 150.

7. Kerman, *Musicology*, 228.

8. This is discussed in the final section of the present chapter.

9. Kerman, *Musicology*, 17.

10. Ibid., 67.

11. Kerman, 'American Musicology in the 1990s', 141; the paragraph discussed is in *Musicology*, 17.

12. In this capacity his stature is of a rather different kind from that of, say, Schenker, whose influence, however great, only extends to musicology. Current work on Schenker, moreover, is trying to show how his ideas are informed by a range of cultural attitudes, whereas such contextualization is intrinsic to Adorno.

13. For more on mediation in musical material, see Paddison, *Adorno's Aesthetics of Music*.

14. Adorno's popular music critique is discussed further in Ch. 4.

15. Adorno's and Horkheimer's *Dialectic of Enlightenment* is discussed in Ch. 6.

16. Kramer, *Franz Schubert*. His reading of 'Die Forelle' is discussed in Ch. 3.

17. Adorno's work on narrative in Mahler is discussed in Ch. 2.

18. Adorno argues that *Philosophy of Modern Music* describes processes in Stravinsky's music, not the state of mind of its composer: 'Stravinsky: A Dialectical Portrait', 148.

19. I owe this point to Bernstein, *The Fate of Art*, 227.

20. For a discussion of Adorno and postmodernism, see my *New Music and the Claims of Modernity*.

21. Hepokoski, 'The Dahlhaus Project and its Extra-musicological Sources'. My account of Dahlhaus is indebted to this persuasive article.

22. Dahlhaus, *Foundations of Music History*, 42.

23. Ibid., 41 and 90.

24. Dahlhaus, *The Idea of Absolute Music*, 2. A similar view is expressed in the preface to *Esthetics of Music*.

25. Dahlhaus, *Schoenberg and the New Music*, 221.

26. Dahlhaus, *Nineteenth-Century Music*, 1.

27. Dahlhaus, *Foundations of Music History*, 157.

28. Gadamer, *Truth and Method*, 303.

29. Ibid., 306.

30. Dahlhaus, *Foundations of Music History*, 70.

31. Ibid., 97.

32. Jauss, *Toward an Aesthetic of Reception*, 33.

33. Dahlhaus, *Foundations of Music History*, 64.

34. Jauss, *Toward an Aesthetic of Reception*, 191.

35. Dahlhaus, *Nineteenth-Century Music*, 7; *Foundations of Music History*, 17.

36. Dahlhaus, *Foundations of Music History*, 157.

37. Hepokoski, 'The Dahlhaus Project', 236.

38. Dahlhaus, *Foundations of Music History*, 116.

39. Ibid., 1.

40. Hepokoski, 'The Dahlhaus Project', 222 and 237.

41. Dahlhaus, *Schoenberg and the New Music*, 243 and 247.

42. Dahlhaus, *Foundations of Music History*, 141–42.

43. Hepokoski, 'The Dahlhaus Project', 237.

Notes to Chapter 2

1. This point is made by Culler, *On Deconstruction*, 24–30.

2. See Monelle's *Linguistics and Semiotics in Music* for a study of musical semiotics.

3. Barthes, *Mythologies*, 38.

4. Lévi-Strauss, *The Origin of Table Manners*, 191.

5. Lévi-Strauss, *The Naked Man*, 182; the myth is discussed in Part III.

6. Ibid., 652.

7. Lévi-Strauss, *The Raw and the Cooked*, 15–16 and 18.

8. This theme is found through the whole of Hanslick's *On the Musically Beautiful*, but see in particular 28–29.

9. For introductions to Schenkerian and other analytical techniques, also see Dunsby and Whittall, *Music Analysis in Theory and Practice* and Cook, *A Guide to Musical Analysis*.

10. See Eco, 'Series and Structure', for more on this distinction.

11. Nattiez, 'Varèse's *Density 21.5*'.

12. See Middleton for discussion of this idea, *Studying Popular Music*, 192–96.

13. Lévi-Strauss, *The Naked Man*, 687.

14. Dews, *Logics of Disintegration*, 77.

15. The phrase is Kramer's, *Classical Music and Postmodern Knowledge*, 6.

16. Van den Toorn, *Music, Politics, and the Academy*, ch. 2.

17. For thoughts on the prospect of systematic and semantic networks intersecting, see Pople, 'Editorial: Allez Forte!'.

18. The phrase paraphrases Derrida's argument in *Positions*; Culler, *On Deconstruction*, 129.

19. Derrida, *Of Grammatology*, 101–40.

20. Ibid., 195–216.

21. De Man, 'The Rhetoric of Blindness: Jacques Derrida's Reading of Rousseau'.

22. Kramer distinguishes between these discourses by talking of 'music as cultural trope' and 'music as cultural object', *Classical Music and Postmodern Knowledge*, 61. For more on organicism, See Street, 'Superior Myths, Dogmatic Allegories'.

23. For discussion of the American reception of Schenker, see Snarrenberg, 'Competing Myths'. For information on the editing of Schenker, see 'Allen Forte to the Editor'; see also Rothstein, 'The Americanization of Heinrich Schenker'.

24. See Snarrenberg, *Schenker's Interpretive Practice*. Spitzer's 'Convergences: Criticism, Analysis and Beethoven Reception' situates Schenker's ideas in a history of music theory.

25. Subotnik, *Deconstuctive Variations*, ch. 2.

26. Ayrey, 'Universe of Particulars', the middleground graph is on pp. 372–73.

27. Lévi-Strauss, *The Raw and the Cooked*, 15.

28. Clément, *Opera, or the Undoing of Women*, 165. For another Lévi-Straussian segmentation of the *The Ring*, focusing on *Siegfried*, see Tarasti, *Myth and Music*, 173–222.

29. Clément, *Opera, or the Undoing of Women*, 165, and Abbate, *Unsung Voices*, 161, both make this point.

30. Dahlhaus, *Richard Wagner's Music Dramas*, 108.

31. Barthes, 'From Work to Text', 156.

32. For a textual discussion of notation, see Cook, *Music: A Very Short Introduction*, ch. 4.

33. For the difficulties encountered in editing Chopin, see ibid., 91.

34. For discussion of new music and theories of modernity, see my *New Music and the Claims of Modernity*.

35. Derrida's essays in this area, along with a summary of Searle's main points, can be found in *Limited Inc*.

36. Deconstruction's interest in the performative has been noted by musicologists, particularly by Kramer, who has applied it to what he calls 'hermeneutic windows'. He argues that by studying music's performative actions, one can compare its strategies with similar procedures in other art-forms with a more obvious semantic content, such as poetry or painting, and thereby wrest meaning from music. See *Music as Cultural Practice*, 7–10.

37. Nattiez makes this point, *Music and Discourse*, 183–84.

38. For discussion of this point, see Kramer, *Classical Music and Postmodern Knowledge*, 13–19.

39. Norris, *What's Wrong with Postmodernism*, 38.

40. This passage is quoted by Norris, ibid., 45 and is taken from Derrida, *Limited Inc*, 137.

41. Nattiez, 'Can one Speak of Narrativity in Music?', 242.

42. For discussion of Berlioz's programmatic account of the Funeral March from Beethoven's *Eroica* Symphony, see Abbate, *Unsung Voices*, 21–23.

43. Abbate makes a similar suggestion, *Unsung Voices*, 26.

44. Newcomb, 'Narrative Archetypes and Mahler's Ninth Symphony', 119.

45. A.B. Marx, *Musical Form in the Age of Beethoven*, ch. 5.

46. See McClary, who quotes Teresa de Lauretis, on the hero in narrative, *Feminine Endings*, 14.

47. On the gap between narrative and music, and the speculative nature of attempts to link them, see Street, 'The Obbligato Recitative', 183, and Samuels, *Mahler's Sixth Symphony*, 164–5.

48. Abbate, *Unsung Voices*, 28–29.

49. Ibid., 151; Abbate's italics.

50. Adorno, *Mahler: A Musical Physiognomy*, 95.

51. Samuels, *Mahler's Sixth Symphony*, 141.

52. Adorno, *Mahler: A Musical Physiognomy*, 76.

53. Tagg, *'Kojak', 50 Seconds of Television Music*, 128–29.

54. White, 'Commentary: Form, Reference, and Ideology in Musical Discourse', 298.

55. Barthes, 'The Death of the Author', 148.

Notes to Chapter 3

1. These figures are all discussed in Bowers and Tick, *Women Making Music*. See also Cook and Tsou, *Cecilia Reclaimed*.

2. See Tick, *Ruth Crawford Seeger*.

3. This point is made by Sandra Gilbert and Susan Gubar, *The Madwoman in the Attic*, 47. They take a lead from Juliet Mitchell's comment that psychoanalysis is not a recommendation *for* a patriarchal society, but an analysis of an existing one.

4. Gilbert and Gubar, *The Madwoman in the Attic*, 49.

5. Straus, *Remaking the Past*, 18.

6. Bowers and Tick, *Women Making Music*, 4.

7. For more on text, authorship and performers, see Ellis, 'The Fair Sax'.

8. Cusick, 'Gender, Musicology, and Feminism', 491.

9. Hanslick, *On the Musically Beautiful*, 29.

10. For a discussion of 'gender and sexuality in musical narrative', see McClary, *Feminine Endings*, 12–17.

11. Quoted in Citron, *Gender and the Musical Canon*, 135.

12. Quoted ibid., 136.

13. McClary, *Feminine Endings*, 9. The reference is to the 1970 edition of the *Harvard Dictionary of Music*.

14. Kallberg, 'The Harmony of the Tea Table', 104.

15. See Babbitt's sleeve notes accompanying the recording of *Philomel*. New World Records NW 307 (1980).

16. McClary, 'Terminal Prestige', 75.

17. Brett, 'Musicality, Essentialism and the Closet', gives various euphemisms for homosexuality, such as the question, 'is he musical?', 11, and the enquiry, 'does he play in the orchestra?', 23 n.

18. Tick, 'Charles Ives and Gender Ideology', 85.

19. Cusick, 'Gender, Musicology, and Feminism', 472.

20. Ibid., 477.

21. See Kramer for discussion of this distinction, *Classical Music*, 61.

22. For more on the policing of masculinity in music criticism, see Biddle, 'Policing Masculinity: Schumann, Berlioz and the Gendering of the Music-Critical Idiom'.

23. Leppert, *The Sight of Sound*, 110–11.

24. See *The Reluctant Pianist*, illustrated ibid., 181.

25. Cixous, 'The Laugh of the Medusa', 338.

26. This defence is mentioned in Solie, 'Introduction: On "Difference"', 5.

27. Quoted in Showalter, 'A Criticism of Our Own', 178.

28. Barthes, 'Rasch', in *The Responsibility of Forms*, 299.

29. Ibid., 302.

30. Silverman, *The Acoustic Mirror*, 191.

31. Ibid., 189. Abbate, 'Opera; or, the Envoicing of Women' also discusses Silverman's reading of late Barthes.

32. Clément, *Opera*, 45.

33. Ibid.

34. Ibid., 179.

35. This reading is found in the final chapter of *Unsung Voices*.

36. Wotan's Monologue is discussed in ch. 5 of *Unsung Voices*.

37. Žižek, 'There is no Sexual Relationship', 214.

38. Pollock, *Vision and Difference*, 75.

39. Abbate tackles this question in 'Opera; or, the Envoicing of Women'.

40. Kramer, *Franz Schubert*, ch. 3.

41. Warhol and Herndl comment: 'Feminist critics generally agree that the oppression of women is a fact of life, that gender leaves its traces in literary texts and on literary history, and that feminist literary criticism plays a worthwhile part in the struggle to end oppression in the world outside of texts.' 'About Feminisms', *Feminisms*, p. x.

42. See Ch. 6 for more on this.

43. This point is argued by Moi, *Sexual/Textual Politics*, 170; and by Kristeva, 'Women's Time', 208.

44. Kristeva, 'Women's Time', 200.

45. Schwarz, *Listening Subjects*, 27.

46. Ibid.

47. Schwarz discusses 'Ihr Bild' in ch. 4 of *Listening Subjects*.

48. Kristeva, 'Revolution in Poetic Language'. Kramer, *Classical Music*, 93–98.

49. Moi, *Sexual/Textual Politics*, 162.

50. Foster, *The Return of the Real*, 149.

51. Žižek offers a Lacanian reading of popular culture in *Looking Awry*, while Foster mentions the fascination with trauma in the television show *Oprah*, see *The Return of the Real*, 168.

52. Foster, *The Return of the Real*, 168.

Notes to Chapter 4

1. There are signs that the study of popular music is becoming less obstinately multidisciplinary and more reciprocally interdisciplinary. Richard Middleton's pioneering *Studying Popular Music* draws on the full range of approaches to the subject; and David Brackett's *Interpreting Popular Music* also combines aspects of musicology and cultural studies.

2. Jameson, *Late Marxism*, 144.

3. Adorno, *Introduction to the Sociology of Music*, 29.

4. For further information on the popular music on which Adorno based his critique, see Middleton, *Studying Popular Music*, ch. 2.

5. Adorno, *Dialectic of Enlightenment*, 125.

6. Adorno, 'Letters to Walter Benjamin', 123.

7. Adorno, *Introduction to the Sociology of Music*, 25.

8. Ibid., 31.

9. Adorno, 'Perennial Fashion—Jazz', 126.

10. For discussion of what Adorno might have known about jazz and how he chose to portray it, see Cooper, 'On *Über Jazz*: Replaying Adorno with the Grain', 123–30.

11. This point is made by Middleton, *Studying Popular Music*, 44.

12. Ibid., 43.

13. *Adorno, Modernism and Mass Culture*, ch. 3.

14. Middleton, *Studying Popular Music*, 66.

15. Williams, 'The Future of Cultural Studies', 151.

16. Hebdige, *Subculture*, 1068.

17. Johnson, 'What is Cultural Studies Anyway?', 97.

18. Covach, 'Popular Music, Unpopular Musicology', 466. He expresses a similar view in 'We Won't Get Fooled Again: Rock Music and Musical Analysis'.

19. For discussion of how sounds are socially situated, See Martin, *Sounds and Society*, 160–66.

20. For a practice of analysis that moves beyond such expectations and 'addresses the organization of sound as part of a broader cultural processes', see Krims, *Rap Music and the Poetics of Identity*, quotation taken from p. 14.

21. This view is put forward by Middleton in *Studying Popular Music*, McClary and Walser, in 'Start Making Sense', and Griffiths, in 'The High Analysis of Low Music'.

22. Lloyd, *Folk Song in England*.

23. This argument is made by Harker, *Fakesong*, 245–53.

24. Bartók, 'The Influence of Peasant Music on Modern Music', 341.

25. This point is made by Taruskin, 'Russian Folk Melodies in *The Rite of Spring*'.

26. Frith, '"The magic that can set you free"', 159.
27. Frith, *Music for Pleasure*, 95.
28. Ibid., 101.
29. As a rock critic, Frith is, not surprisingly, elsewhere critical of Adorno's position, making the familiar (though necessary) point that, 'the actual use of music by pop fans is scarcely examined', though Springsteen's fans appear to accept the contradiction they are offered. Frith, *Sound Effects*, 45.
30. Frith, *Performing Rites*, 20.
31. Frith, *Music for Pleasure*, 72.
32. This theme is pursued by Eyerman and Jamison, *Music and Social Movements*, 124–30.
33. Bob Dylan, *Blood on the Tracks* (Columbia, 1975).
34. This point is made by Lhamon, 'A Cut Above', 196.
35. This point is made by Griffiths, 'The High Analysis of Low Music', 418. This article also contains an interesting discussion of Shawn Colvin's cover version of 'You're Gonna Make Me Lonesome When You Go', from the same album.
36. This observation is made by Ricks, 'Clichés and American English', 166.
37. This point is made by Negus (paraphrasing Frith), *Popular Music in Theory*, 149.
38. See Negus for discussion of this point, ibid., 151.
39. This point is made by Negus, following Peter Wicke, ibid., 152–53.
40. Frith, 'Afterthoughts', 421.
41. See Fink for discussion of sexuality in Presley's 'Hound Dog', in 'Elvis Everywhere', 169–75.
42. Frith and McRobbie, 'Rock and Sexuality', 374.
43. Ibid., 381.
44. McRobbie, 'Settling Accounts with Subcultures'.
45. Frith, 'Afterthoughts', 422.
46. Walser, *Running with the Devil*, 132–33.
47. Tagg, 'Open Letter: "Black music", "Afro-American music" and "European music"', 289.
48. Brackett, *Interpreting Popular Music*, ch. 4.
49. Gilroy, *The Black Atlantic*, 99.
50. Ibid., 96.
51. For more discussion along these lines, see Hutnyk, 'Adorno at Womad'.
52. McClary makes the comparison, *Feminine Endings*, 149.
53. All Madonna music-videos mentioned are on 'Madonna: The Immaculate Collection' (Warner Music Vision, 1990).
54. Fiske, 'British Cultural Studies and Television', 312.
55. Bordo, '"Material Girl": The Effacements of Postmodern Culture', 1110.
56. Goodwin, *Dancing in the Distraction Factory*.
57. The lyrics are quoted in Cook, *Analysing Musical Multimedia*, 152.
58. For an analysis of music and image in 'Material Girl', see, ibid., ch. 4.
59. Frith, *Performing Rites*, 213.
60. *The Best of Dolly Parton* (BMG Entertainment International, 1997).
61. Mockus, 'Queer Thoughts on Country Music and k.d. lang', 265.
62. Mockus also mentions the 'I–You' mode of address, ibid., 261.

63. k.d. lang/Ben Mink (Bumstead Publishing/Zavion Music, 1989) recorded on *Absolute Torch and Twang*, Sire Records.

64. For more on subjectivity in dance music, see Toynbee, *Making Popular Music*, ch. 5.

65. Frith, *Performing Rites*, 272.

66. I am drawing on comments made ibid., 20 and 275.

Notes to Chapter 5

1. For discussion of critical responses to *Orientalism*, see Moore-Gilbert, *Postcolonial Theory*.

2. Ibid., 39.

3. For discussion of artistic representations of the Middle East, See Locke, 'Constructing the Oriental "Other"', 271 and 280.

4. Ibid., 271.

5. Ibid., 267.

6. Said, *Culture and Imperialism*, 134.

7. Ibid., 156.

8. Robinson, 'Is *Aida* an Orientalist Opera?'.

9. Locke makes this point in 'Cutthroats and Casbah Dancers', 50.

10. Kramer, *Classical Music and Postmodern Knowledge*, 216.

11. Ibid., 225.

12. Ibid., 204.

13. Merriam, *The Anthropology of Music*, 319.

14. For this development, see Merriam, 'Definitions of "Comparative Musicology" and "Ethnomusicology"'.

15. Shelemay, 'Crossing Boundaries in Music', 21. A similar point is made by Jonathan Stock, 'New Musicologies, Old Musicologies', 40–41.

16. For more on what anthropology brings to the study of music, see Qureshi, 'Music Anthropologies and Music Histories', 333.

17. Rice, 'Toward a Remodeling of Ethnomusicology', 476.

18. Tomlinson, 'The Web of Culture', 351.

19. Graphic methods, such as the melograph, try to bypass the limitations of notation.

20. Bohlman, 'Ontologies of Music', 20.

21. Bhabha, *The Location of Culture*, 12.

22. Stokes makes this point, Introduction to *Ethnicity, Identity and Music*, 9.

23. Nettl, 'The Institutionalization of Musicology', 305.

24. Bohlman makes similar points, 'Ethnomusicology's Challenge', 131.

25. Nettl, 'The Institutionalization of Musicology', 305.

26. For more on this shift, see Cooley, 'Casting Shadows in the Field', 11.

27. Rice, 'Toward a Mediation of Field Methods and Field Experience in Ethnomusicology', 116.

28. Babiracki, 'What's the Difference?', 127.

29. Ibid., 132.

30. Koskoff, 'What Do We Want to Teach When We Teach Music?', 546.

31. Rice, 'Toward a Mediation of Field Methods and Field Experience in Ethnomusicology', 116–17.

32. Ibid., 119.
33. Bohlman, *The Study of Folk Music in the Modern World*, 120–24.
34. Bohlman makes this point, 'Immigrant, Folk and Regional Musics in the Twentieth Century', 299.
35. Bhabha, *The Location of Culture*, 6.
36. This point is made by Giddens, *The Consequences of Modernity*, 175.
37. See Chapter 2 for a discussion of Derrida's readings of Rousseau and Lévi-Strauss.

Notes to Chapter 6

1. These themes are explored by Giddens in *The Consequences of Modernity*, particularly in the first section.
2. Adorno and Horkheimer, *Dialectic of Enlightenment*, 32–5.
3. See the chapter on Adorno in Habermas's *The Philosophical Discourse of Modernity*.
4. For discussion of Foucault reception, see Gutting, *The Cambridge Companion to Foucault*.
5. For discussion of various readings of Derrida, including Norris's own, see Norris, 'Limited Think: How not to Read Derrida', in *What's Wrong with Postmodernism*.
6. Feminism and post-Enlightenment rationalism are discussed in Ch. 3.
7. Lyotard's views on grand narrative are to be found in *The Postmodern Condition*, 27–37.
8. For discussion of globalization, see Giddens, *The Consequences of Modernity*.
9. These contradictions are discussed in Manuel, 'Music as Symbol, Music as Simulacrum'.
10. Haraway, *Simians, Cyborgs, and Women*, 191.
11. Ibid., 196.
12. The original article was published in *Repercussions*, 1 (1992). The Kramer/Tomlinson debate is contained in *Current Musicology*, 53 (1993).
13. Kramer, *Classical Music and Postmodern Knowledge*, 3 and 5.
14. Ibid., 7.
15. Ibid., p. xiv.
16. Tomlinson, 'Musical Pasts and Postmodern Musicologies: A Response to Lawrence Kramer', 23.
17. These overlaps are discussed in ch. 1 of *Music in Renaissance Magic*.
18. Tomlinson, 'Musical Pasts and Postmodern Musicologies', 20.
19. Ibid., 22.
20. See Samson on the irreducible in music, 'Analysis in Context', 47.
21. Tomlinson, 'Musical Pasts and Postmodern Musicologies', 23.
22. Kramer, 'Music Criticism and the Postmodernist Turn: In Contrary Motion with Gary Tomlinson', 32.
23. Veeser, *The New Historicism Reader*, 2.
24. Kramer, *Music as Cultural Practice*, 17.
25. Leppert, *The Sight of Sound*.
26. Kramer, *Classical Music and Postmodern Knowledge*, 25.

27. Babbitt, 'The Composer as Specialist'.

28. For discussion of the institutionalization of modernism, see Born, *Rationalizing Culture*.

29. See 'Putting the Phantoms to Flight' in *Orientations*.

30. For analysis of system and disintegration in Boulez and Cage, and discussion of inclusive composition, particularly Rihm, see my *New Music and the Claims of Modernity*.

31. This argument is made in my 'Adorno and the Semantics of Modernism'.

32. Jencks discusses and illustrates the Clore Gallery in 'The Emergent Rules', 283–84; it also appears in his *The Language of Post-Modern Architecture*, 142.

33. For more details on this project, see Whiteread, *House*.

34. Foster, *The Return of the Real*, 148; also contains illustrations.

35. Jameson, *Postmodernism, or, the Cultural Logic of Late Capitalism*, p. x.

36. For more on what he calls 'the imminent collapse of the cultural authority of the classical music canon', see Fink, 'Elvis Everywhere', 138.

37. Cook, *Analysing Musical Multimedia*, 4–9.

38. Richard Strauss, *Ein Heldenleben*, Op. 40 (Deutsche Grammophon, 1959), BPO, Karajan.

39. The idea that authentic performance is a modern performance style is the main theme of Taruskin's *Text and Act*.

40. Hoffmann, 'Beethoven's Instrumental Music', 152.

41. Wagner, 'On Conducting', 63.

42. Hanslick, 'Brahms's Symphony No. 3', 211.

43. For discussion of Schenker's metaphors, see Snarrenberg, 'Competing Myths'.

44. Tovey, 'Beethoven, Symphony in C minor', 56.

45. See in particular the last chapter of Burnham's *Beethoven Hero*.

46. Kramer, *Classical Music and Postmodern Knowledge*, 25.

47. Schenker notes that the oboe cadenza corresponds to bars 22–24, thereby examining its structural rather than poetic significance.

48. This point is made by Kramer, *Music and Poetry*, 234–41.

49. Burnham, 'How Music Matters: Poetic Content Revisited', 202–8.

50. Quoted ibid., 205.

51. Ibid., 208.

52. Derrida, *Specters of Marx*.

53. This point is made by Burnham, *Beethoven Hero*, 162.

54. See the final chapter of Scruton's *Aesthetics of Music* for a recent defence of bourgeois values.

Bibliography

Abbate, Carolyn, 'Opera; or, the Envoicing of Women', in Solie (ed.), *Musicology and Difference*, 225–58.

——, *Unsung Voices: Opera and Musical Narrative in the Nineteenth Century* (Princeton: Princeton University Press, 1991).

Adler, Guido, 'Umfang, Methode und Ziel der Musikwissenschaft', *Vierteljahrsschrift für Musikwissenschaft*, 1 (1885).

Adorno T.W., *Aesthetic Theory*, trans. Robert Hullot-Kentor (London: Athlone Press, 1997).

——, *Alban Berg: Master of the Smallest Link*, trans. Juliane Brand and Christopher Hailey (Cambridge: Cambridge University Press, 1991).

——, *Beethoven: The Philosophy of Music*, ed. Rolf Tiedemann, trans. Edmund Jephcott (Stanford, Calif.: Stanford University Press, 1998).

——, *In Search of Wagner*, trans. Rodney Livingstone (London: Verso, 1981).

——, *Introduction to the Sociology of Music*, trans. E.B. Ashton (New York: Seabury Press, 1976).

——, 'Letters to Walter Benjamin', trans. H. Zohn, *Aesthetics and Politics* (London: Verso, 1977).

——, *Mahler: A Musical Physiognomy*, trans. Edmund Jephcott (Chicago: University of Chicago Press, 1992).

——, 'Perennial Fashion—Jazz', in *Prisms*, 119–32.

——, *Philosophy of Modern Music*, trans. Anne Mitchell and Wesley Bloomster (London: Sheed & Ward, 1973).

——, *Prisms*, trans. Samuel and Shierry Weber (Cambridge, Mass.: MIT Press, 1981).

——, 'Stravinsky: A Dialectical Portrait', *Quasi una fantasia: Essays on Modern Music*, trans. Rodney Livingstone (London: Verso, 1992), 145–75.

—— and Max Horkheimer, *Dialectic of Enlightenment*, trans. John Cumming (London: Verso, 1972).

Austin, J.L., *How to Do Things with Words* (Cambridge, Mass.: Harvard University Press, 1975).

Ayrey, Craig, 'Universe of Particulars', *Music Analysis*, 17/3 (1998), 339–81.

Babbitt, Milton, 'The Composer as Specialist', in Richard Kostelanetz (ed.), *Esthetics Contemporary* (New York: Prometheus Books, 19678), 280–87.

Babiracki, Carol, 'What's the Difference? Reflections on Gender and Research in Village India', in Barz and Cooley (eds), *Shadows in the Field*, 121–36.

Barthes, Roland, 'The Death of the Author', in *Image-Music-Text*, 142–48.

——, 'From Work to Text', in *Image-Music-Text*, 155–64.

——, 'The Grain of the Voice', in *Image-Music-Text*, 179–89.

——, *Image-Music-Text*, trans. Stephen Heath (London: Fontana, 1977).

——, *Mythologies*, trans. Annette Lavers (London: Jonathan Cape, 1972).

——, 'Rasch', in *The Responsibility of Forms*, trans. R. Howard (Oxford: Blackwell, 1985), 299–312.

Bartók, Béla, 'The Influence of Peasant Music on Modern Music', in *Bela Bartók's Essays*, ed. Benjamin Suchoff (London: Faber, 1976), 340–44.

Barz, Gregory, and Timothy Cooley, *Shadows in the Field: New Perspectives for Fieldwork in Ethnomusicology* (New York and Oxford: Oxford University Press, 1997).

Benjamin, Walter, *The Arcades Project*, trans. Howard Eiland and Kevin McLaughlin (Harvard: Harvard University Press, 1999).

——, 'The Work of Art in the Age of Mechanical Reproduction', in Hannah Arendt (ed.), *Illuminations: Essays and Reflections* (New York: Schocken Books, 1969), 217–51.

Bernstein, J. M., *The Fate of Art: Aesthetic Alienation from Kant to Derrida and Adorno* (Cambridge: Polity Press, 1993).

Bhabha, Homi, *The Location of Culture* (London: Routledge, 1994).

Biddle, Ian, 'Policing Masculinity: Schumann, Berlioz and the Gendering of the Music-Critical Idiom', *Journal of the Royal Musical Association*, 124/2 (1999), 196–220.

Bloom, Harold, *The Anxiety of Influence: A Theory of Poetry* (Oxford: Oxford University Press, 1973).

Bohlman, Philip, 'Ethnomusicology's Challenge to the Canon; The Canon's Challenge to Ethnomusicology', in Katherine Bergeron and Philip Bohlman (eds), *Disciplining Music: Musicology and its Canons* (Chicago and London: University of Chicago Press, 1992).

——, 'Immigrant, Folk, and Regional Musics in the Twentieth Century', in David Nicholls (ed.), *The Cambridge History of American Music* (Cambridge: Cambridge University Press, 1998), 276–308.

——, 'Ontologies of Music', in Cook and Everist (eds), *Rethinking Music*, 17–34.

——, *The Study of Folk Music in the Modern World* (Bloomington and Indianapolis: Indiana University Press, 1988).

Bordo, Susan, '"Material Girl": The Effacements of Postmodern Culture', in Julie Rivkin and Michael Ryan (eds), *Literary Theory: An Anthology* (Oxford: Blackwell, 1998), 1099–1115.

Born, Georgina, *Rationalizing Culture: IRCAM, Boulez, and the Institutionalization of the Avant-garde* (Berkeley: University of California Press, 1995).

Boulez, Pierre, *Orientations: Collected Writings by Pierre Boulez*, ed. Jean-Jacques Nattiez, trans. Martin Cooper (London: Faber, 1986).

Bowers, Jane and Judith Tick (eds), *Women Making Music: The Western Art Tradition*, 1150–1950 (Urbana and Chicago: University of Illinois Press, 1986).

Brackett, David, *Interpreting Popular Music* (Cambridge: Cambridge University Press, 1995).

Brett, Philip, 'Musicality, Essentialism, and the Closet', in Brett, Wood and Thomas (eds), *Queering the Pitch*, 9–26.

——, Elizabeth Wood and Gary C. Thomas (eds), *Queering the Pitch: The New Lesbian and Gay Musicology* (New York: Routledge, 1994).

Burnham, Scott, *Beethoven Hero* (Princeton: Princeton University Press, 1995).

——, 'How Music Matters: Poetic Content Revisited', in Cook and Everist (eds), *Rethinking Music*, 193–216.

Chua, Daniel, *Absolute Music and the Construction of Meaning* (Cambridge: Cambridge University Press, 1999).

Citron, Marcia, *Gender and the Musical Canon* (Cambridge: Cambridge University Press, 1993).

Cixous, Hélène, 'The Laugh of the Medusa', in Warhol and Herndl (eds.), *Feminisms*, 334–49.

Clément, Catherine, *Opera, or the Undoing of Women*, trans. Betsy Wing (Minneapolis: University of Minnesota Press, 1988).

Cook, Nicholas, *Analysing Musical Multimedia* (Oxford: Clarendon Press, 1998).

——, *A Guide to Musical Analysis* (London: Dent, 1987).

——, *Music: A Very Short Introduction* (Oxford: Oxford University Press, 1998).

—— and Mark Everist (eds), *Rethinking Music* (Oxford: Oxford University Press, 1999).

Cook, Susan, and Judy Tsou (eds), *Cecilia Reclaimed: Feminist Perspectives on Gender and Music* (Urbana and Chicago: University of Illinois Press, 1994).

Cooley, Timothy, 'Casting Shadows in the Field', in Barz and Cooley (eds), *Shadows in the Field*, 3–19.

Cooper, Harry, 'On *Über Jazz*: Replaying Adorno with the Grain', *October*, 75 (1996), 99–133.

Covach, John, 'Popular Music, Unpopular Musicology', in Cook and Everist (eds), *Rethinking Music*, 452–70.

——, 'We Won't Get Fooled Again: Rock Music and Musical Analysis', *In Theory Only*, 13 (1997), 110–37.

Culler, Jonathan, *Literary Theory: A Very Short Introduction* (Oxford: Oxford University Press, 1997).

——, *On Deconstruction: Theory and Criticism after Structuralism* (Ithaca, NY: Cornell University Press, 1982).

Cusick, Suzanne, 'Gender, Musicology, and Feminism', in Cook and Everist (eds), *Rethinking Music*, 471–98.

Dahlhaus, Carl, *Esthetics of Music*, trans. William Austin (Cambridge: Cambridge University Press, 1982).

——, *Foundations of Music History*, trans. J.B. Robinson (Cambridge: Cambridge University Press, 1983).

——, *The Idea of Absolute Music*, trans. Roger Lustig (Chicago: University of Chicago Press, 1989).

——, *Nineteenth-Century Music*, trans. J. Bradford Robinson (Berkeley, University of California Press, 1989).

——, *Richard Wagner's Music Dramas*, trans. Mary Whittall (Cambridge: Cambridge University Press, 1979).

Dahlhaus, Carl, *Schoenberg and the New Music*, trans. Derrick Puffett and Alfred Clayton (Cambridge: Cambridge University Press, 1987).

De Man, Paul, 'The Rhetoric of Blindness: Jacques Derrida's Reading of Rousseau', in *Blindness and Insight: Essays in the Rhetoric of Contemporary Criticism* (London: Methuen, 1986), 102–41.

Derrida, Jacques, *Limited Inc*, trans. Samuel Weber *et al.* (Evanston, Ill.: Northwestern University Press, 1989).

——, *Of Grammatology*, trans. Gayatri Chakravorty Spivak (Baltimore: The Johns Hopkins University Press, 1974).

——, *Positions*, trans. Alan Bass (London: Athlone Press, 1981).

——, *Specters of Marx*, trans. Peggy Kamuf (London: Routledge, 1994).

Dews, Peter, *Logics of Disintegration: Post-Structuralist Thought and the Claims of Critical Theory* (London: Verso, 1987).

Dunsby, Jonathan, and Arnold Whittall, *Music Analysis in Theory and Practice* (London: Faber, 1988).

Eagleton, Terry, *The Illusions of Postmodernism* (Oxford: Blackwell, 1996).

Eco, Umberto, 'Series and Structure', in *The Open Work*, trans. Anna Cancogni (Cambridge, Mass.: Harvard University Press, 1989), 217–35.

Ellis, Katharine, 'The Fair Sax', *Journal of the Royal Musical Association*, 124/2 (1999), 221–54.

Eyerman, Ron, and Andrew Jamison, *Music and Social Movements: Mobilizing Traditions in the Twentieth Century* (Cambridge: Cambridge University Press, 1998).

Fink, Robert, 'Elvis Everywhere: Musicology and Popular Music Studies at the Twilight of the Canon', *American Music*, 16/2 (1998), 135–79.

Fiske, John, 'British Cultural Studies and Television', in Robert Allen (ed.), *Channels of Discourse, Reassembled* (London: Routledge, 1992), 284–326.

Forte, Allen, 'Allen Forte to the Editor', *Music Analysis*, 17/2 (1998), 261–3.

—— and Stephen Gilbert, *An Introduction to Schenkerian Analysis* (New York & London: Norton, 1982).

Foster, Hal, *The Return of the Real* (Cambridge, Mass.: MIT Press, 1996).

Frith, Simon, 'Afterthoughts', in Frith and Goodwin (eds), *On Record: Rock, Pop, and the Written Word*, 419–24.

——, '"The magic that can set you free": The Ideology of the Folk and the Myth of the Rock Community', *Popular Music*, 1 (1981), 159–68.

——, *Music for Pleasure* (Cambridge: Polity Press, 1988).

——, *Performing Rites: On the Value of Popular Music* (Oxford: Oxford University Press, 1996).

——, *Sound Effects* (New York: Pantheon Books, 1981).

—— and Andrew Goodwin (eds), *On Record: Rock, Pop, and the Written Word* (London: Routledge, 1990).

—— and Angela McRobbie, 'Rock and Sexuality', in Frith and Goodwin (eds), *On Record: Rock, Pop, and the Written Word*, 371–89.

Gadamer, Hans-Georg, *Truth and Method*, trans. revised by Joel Weinsheimer and Donald G. Marshall (London: Sheed and Ward Ltd, 1989).

Giddens, Anthony, *The Consequences of Modernity* (Cambridge: Polity Press, 1990).

Gilbert, Sandra, and Susan Gubar, *The Madwoman in the Attic* (New Haven and London: Yale University Press, 1979).

Gilroy, Paul, *The Black Atlantic: Modernity and Double-Consciousness* (London: Verso, 1993).

Goodwin, Andrew, *Dancing in the Distraction Factory: Music, TV and Popular Culture* (Minnesota: University of Minnesota Press, 1992).

Griffiths, Dai, 'The High Analysis of Low Music', *Music Analysis*, 18/3 (1999), 389–435.

Gutting, Gary (ed.), *The Cambridge Companion to Foucault* (Cambridge: Cambridge University Press, 1994.

Habermas, Jürgen, 'Modernity—An Incomplete Project', in Hal Foster (ed.), *Postmodern Culture* (London: Pluto Press, 1985), 3–15.

——, *The Philosophical Discourse of Modernity*, trans. Frederick Lawrence (Cambridge: Polity Press, 1987).

Hanslick, Eduard, 'Brahms's Symphony No. 3', in *Music Criticisms 1846–99*, trans. Henry Pleasants (London: Penguin, 1950), 210–13.

——, *On the Musically Beautiful*, trans. Geoffrey Payzant (Indianapolis, Ind.: Hackett Publishing Co., 1986).

Haraway, Donna, *Simians, Cyborgs, and Women: The Reinvention of Nature* (London: Free Association Books, 1991).

Harker, Dave, *Fakesong: The Manufacture of British 'Folksong', 1700 to the Present Day* (Milton Keynes: Open University Press, 1985).

Hebdige, Dick, *Subculture: The Meaning of Style*, extracted in Julie Rivkin and Michael Ryan (eds), *Literary Theory: An Anthology* (Oxford: Blackwell, 1998), 1065–75.

Hepokoski, James, 'The Dahlhaus Project and its Extra-musicological Sources', *19th-Century Music*, 14/3 (1991), 221–48.

Hoffmann, E.T.A., 'Beethoven's Instrumental Music', in Oliver Strunk, *Source Readings in Music History: The Romantic Era* (London: Faber, 1981), 35–41.

Hutnyk, John, 'Adorno at Womad: South Asian Crossovers and the Limits of Hybridity-Talk', in Pnina Werbmer and Tariq Modood (eds), *Debating Cultural Hybridity: Multi-Cultural Identities and the Politics of Anti-Racism* (London: Zed Books, 1997), 106–36.

Huyssen, Andreas, *After the Great Divide* (Basingstoke: Macmillan Press, 1986).

Jameson, Fredric, *Late Marxism: Adorno, or, the Persistence of the Dialectic* (London: Verso, 1990).

——, *Postmodernism, or, the Cultural Logic of Late Capitalism* (London: Verso, 1991).

Jauss, Hans Robert, *Toward an Aesthetic of Reception*, trans. Timothy Bahti (Minneapolis: University of Minnesota Press, 1982).

Jencks, Charles, 'The Emergent Rules', in Thomas Docherty (ed.), *Postmodernism: A Reader* (Hemel Hempstead: Harvester Wheatsheaf, 1993), 281–94.

——, *The Language of Post-Modern Architecture* (London: Academy Editions, 1991).

Johnson, Richard, 'What is Cultural Studies Anyway?', in John Storey (ed.), *What is Cultural Studies? A Reader* (London: Arnold, 1996), 75–114.

Kallberg, Jeffrey, 'The Harmony of the Tea Table: Gender and Ideology in the Piano Nocturne', *Representations*, 39 (1992), 102–33.

Kerman, Joseph, 'American Musicology in the 1990s', *Journal of Musicology*, 9/2 (1991), 131–44.

——, 'A Few Canonic Variations', in Kerman, *Write all These Down*, 33–50.

——, 'How We Got into Analysis, and How to Get Out', in Kerman, *Write all These Down*, 12–32.

——, *Musicology* [*Contemplating Music* in the USA] (London: Fontana Press/Collins, 1985).

——, *Write all These Down* (Berkeley: University of California Press, 1994).

Koskoff, Ellen, 'What Do We Want to Teach When We Teach Music? One Apology, Two Short Trips, Three Ethical Dilemmas, and Eighty-Two Questions', in Cook and Everist (eds), *Rethinking Music*, 545–59.

Kramer, Lawrence, *Classical Music and Postmodern Knowledge* (Berkeley: University of California Press, 1995).

——, *Music and Poetry: The Nineteenth-Century and After* (Berkeley: California, 1984).

——, *Music as Cultural Practice, 1800–1900* (Berkeley: University of California Press, 1990).

——, 'Music Criticism and the Postmodernist Turn: In Contrary Motion with Gary Tomlinson', *Current Musicology*, 53 (1993), 25–35.

——, 'The Musicology of the Future', *Repercussions*, 1 (1992), 5–18.

——, *Franz Schubert: Sexuality, Subjectivity, Song* (Cambridge: Cambridge University Press, 1998).

Krims, Adam, *Rap Music and the Poetics of Identity* (Cambridge: Cambridge University Press, 2000).

Kristeva, Julia, 'Revolution in Poetic Language', trans. Margaret Waller, in Toril Moi (ed.), *The Kristeva Reader* (Oxford: Blackwell, 1986), 89–136.

——, 'Women's Time', trans. Alice Jardine and Harry Blake, in Toril Moi (ed.), *The Kristeva Reader* (Oxford: Blackwell, 1986), 187–213.

Lacan, Jacques, *Écrits: A Selection*, trans. Alan Sheridan (London: Tavistock/Routledge, 1977).

Leppert, Richard, *The Sight of Sound: Music, Representation, and the History of the Body* (Berkeley: University of California Press, 1993).

Lévi-Strauss, Claude, *The Naked Man*, trans. John and Doreen Weightman (London: Jonathan Cape, 1981).

——, *The Origin of Table Manners*, trans. John and Doreen Weightman (London: Jonathan Cape, 1978).

——, *The Raw and the Cooked*, trans. John and Doreen Weightman (London: Jonathan Cape, 1969).

——, *Structural Anthropology*, trans. Claire Jacobson and Brooke Grundfest Schoepf (London: Penguin, 1973).

Lhamon, W.T., Jr, 'A Cut Above', in Elizabeth Thomson & David Gutman (eds), *The Dylan Companion* (London: Papermac, 1990), 195–98.

Lloyd, A.L., *Folk Song in England* (London: Lawrence & Wishart, 1975).

Locke, Ralph, 'Constructing the Oriental "Other": Saint-Saëns' *Samson et Dalila*', *Cambridge Opera Journal*, 3/3 (1991), 261–302.

——, 'Cutthroats and Casbah Dancers, Muezzins and Timeless Sands: Musical Images of the Middle East', *19th-Century Music* 22/1 (1998), 20–53.

Lyotard, Jean-François, *The Postmodern Condition: A Report on Knowledge*, trans. Geoff Bennington and Brian Massumi (Manchester: Manchester University Press, 1984).

Manuel, Peter, 'Music as Symbol, Music as Simulacrum: Postmodern, Premodern and Modern Aesthetics in Subcultural Popular Musics', *Popular Music* 13/3 (1995), 227–39.

Martin, Pete, *Sounds and Society: Themes in the Sociology of Music* (Manchester: Manchester University Press, 1995).

Marx, A.B., *Musical Form in the Age of Beethoven*, ed. and trans. Scott Burnham (Cambridge: Cambridge University Press, 1997).

McClary, Susan, *Feminine Endings: Music, Gender, and Sexuality* (Minneapolis: University of Minnesota Press, 1991).

——, 'Reshaping a Discipline: Musicology and Feminism in the 1990s', *Feminist Studies*, 19 (1992), 399–423.

——, '"Terminal Prestige": The Case of Avant-Garde Music Composition', *Cultural Critique*, 12 (1989), 57–81.

—— and Robert Walser, 'Start Making Sense! Musicology Wrestles with Rock', in Frith and Goodwin (eds), *On Record: Rock, Pop, and the Written Word*, 277–92.

McRobbie, Angela, 'Settling Accounts with Subcultures: A Feminist Critique', in Frith and Goodwin (eds), *On Record: Rock, Pop, and the Written Word*, 66–80.

Merriam, Alan P., *The Anthropology of Music* (Evanston, Ill.: Northwestern University Press, 1964).

——, 'Definitions of "Comparative Musicology" and "Ethnomusicology": An Historical-Theoretical Perspective', *Ethnomusicology*, 21 (1977), 189–204.

Middleton, Richard, *Studying Popular Music* (Milton Keynes: Open University Press, 1990).

Mockus, Martha, 'Queer Thoughts on Country Music and k.d. lang', in Brett, Wood and Thomas (eds), *Queering the Pitch*, 257–71.

Moi, Toril, *Sexual/Textual Politics: Feminist Literary Theory* (London: Routledge, 1985).

Monelle, Raymond, *Linguistics and Semiotics in Music* (New York: Harwood Academic Publishers, 1992).

Moore-Gilbert, Bart, *Postcolonial Theory: Contexts, Practices, Politics* (London: Verso, 1997).

Nattiez, Jean-Jacques, 'Can One Speak of Narrativity in Music?', trans. Katharine Ellis, *Journal of the Royal Musical Association*, 115/2 (1990), 240–57.

——, *Music and Discourse: Toward a Semiology of Music*, trans. Carolyn Abbate (Princeton: Princeton University Press, 1990).

——, 'Varèse's *Density 21.5*: A Study in Semiological Analysis', trans. A. Barry, *Music Analysis* 1/3 (1982), 243–340.

Negus, Keith, *Popular Music in Theory: An Introduction* (Cambridge: Polity Press, 1996).

Nettl, Bruno, 'The Institutionalization of Musicology: Perspectives of a North American Ethnomusicologist', Cook and Everist (eds), *Rethinking Music*, 287–310.

Newcomb, Anthony, 'Narrative Archetypes and Mahler's Ninth Symphony', in Steven Scher (ed.), *Music and Text: Critical Inquiries* (Cambridge: Cambridge University Press, 1992), 118–36.

Norris, Christopher, *What's Wrong with Postmodernism* (Hemel Hempstead: Harvester Wheatsheaf, 1990).

Paddison, Max, *Adorno, Modernism and Mass Culture: Essays on Critical Theory and Music* (London: Kahn & Averill, 1996).

——, *Adorno's Aesthetics of Music* (Cambridge: Cambridge University Press, 1995).

Pollock, Griselda, *Vision and Difference: Femininity, Feminism and the Histories of Art* (London: Routledge, 1988).

Pople, Anthony, 'Editorial: Allez Forte!', *Music Analysis*, 17/2 (1998), 123–26.

—— (ed.), *Theory, Analysis and Meaning in Music* (Cambridge: Cambridge University Press, 1994).

Powers, Harold, 'Language Models and Musical Analysis', *Ethnomusicology*, 24 (1980), 1–60.

Proulx, Annie, *Accordion Crimes* (London: Fourth Estate Limited, 1996).

Qureshi, Regula Burckhardt, 'Music Anthropologies and Music Histories: A Preface and an Agenda', *Journal of the American Musicological Society*, 43 (1995), 31–42.

Rice, Timothy, 'Toward a Mediation of Field Methods and Field Experience in Ethnomusicology', in Barz and Cooley (eds), *Shadows in the Field*, 101–20.

——, 'Toward a Remodeling of Ethnomusicology', *Ethnomusicology*, 31/3 (1987), 469–88.

Ricks, Christopher, 'Clichés and American English', in Elizabeth Thomson and David Gutman (eds), *The Dylan Companion* (London: Papermac, 1990), 163–72.

Robinson, Paul, 'Is Aida an Orientalist Opera?', *Cambridge Opera Journal*, 5/2 (1993), 133–40.

Rothstein, William, 'The Americanization of Heinrich Schenker', in Hedi Siegel (ed.), *Schenker Studies* (Cambridge: Cambridge University Press, 1990), 193–203.

Said, Edward, *Culture and Imperialism* (London: Chatto & Windus, 1993).

——, *Orientalism* (New York: Vintage Books, 1978).

Samson, Jim, 'Analysis in Context', in Cook and Everist (eds), *Rethinking Music*, 35–54.

Samuels, Robert, *Mahler's Sixth Symphony* (Cambridge: Cambridge University Press, 1995).

Saussure, Ferdinand de, *Course in General Linguistics*, trans. Wade Baskin (London: Fontana, 1974).

Schenker, Heinrich, 'Beethoven's Fifth Symphony', in *Beethoven: Symphony No. 5 in C Minor*, ed. E. Forbes (New York: Norton, 1971), 164–82.

Schwarz, David, *Listening Subjects: Music, Psychoanalysis, Culture* (Durham, NC: Duke University Press, 1997).

Scruton, Roger, *The Aesthetics of Music* (New York: Oxford University Press, 1997).

Sharp, Cecil, *English Folk Song: Some Conclusions* (Wakefield: EP Publishing, 1972).

Shelemay, Kay Kaufman, 'Crossing Boundaries in Music and Music Scholarship: A Perspective from Ethnomusicology', *Musical Quarterly*, 80/1 (1996), 13–30.

Showalter, Elaine, 'A Criticism of Our Own: Autonomy and Assimilation in Afro-American and Feminist Literary Theory', in Warhol and Herndl (eds), *Feminisms*, 168–88.

Silverman, Kaja, *The Acoustic Mirror: The Female Voice in Psychoanalysis and Cinema* (Bloomington: Indiana University Press, 1988).

Snarrenberg, Robert, 'Competing Myths: The American Abandonment of Schenker's Organicism', in Pople (ed.), *Theory, Analysis and Meaning in Music*, 29–56.

——, *Schenker's Interpretive Practice* (Cambridge: Cambridge University Press, 1997).

Solie, Ruth, 'Introduction: On "Difference"', in Solie (ed.), *Musicology and Difference.*

—— (ed.), *Musicology and Difference: Gender and Sexuality in Music Scholarship* (Berkeley: University of California Press, 1993), 1–20.

Spitzer, Michael, 'Convergences: Criticism, Analysis and Beethoven Reception', *Music Analysis*, 16/3 (1997), 369–91.

Stock, Jonathan, 'New Musicologies, Old Musicologies: Ethnomusicology and the Study of Western Music', *Current Musicology*, 62 (1999), 40–68.

Stokes, Martin, Introduction, in Martin Stokes (ed.), *Ethnicity, Identity and Music* (Oxford: Berg, 1994), 1–27.

Straus, Joseph N., *Remaking the Past: Musical Modernism and the Influence of the Tonal Tradition* (Cambridge, Mass.: Harvard University Press, 1990).

Street, Alan, 'The Obbligato Recitative: Narrative and Schoenberg's Five Orchestral Pieces, Op. 16', in Pople (ed.), *Theory, Analysis and Meaning in Music*, 164–83.

——, 'Superior Myths, Dogmatic Allegories: The Resistance to Musical Unity', *Music Analysis*, 8/1–2 (1989), 77–123.

Subotnik, Rose Rosengard, *Deconstructive Variations: Music and Reason in Western Society* (Minneapolis: University of Minnesota Press, 1996).

Tagg, Philip, *'Kojak', 50 Seconds of Television Music: Toward the Analysis of Affect in Popular Music* (Gothenberg: Studies from the Department of Musicology, 2, 1979).

——, 'Open Letter: "Black Music", "Afro-American Music" and "European music"', *Popular Music*, 8/3 (1989), 285–98.

Tarasti, Eero, *Myth and Music* (The Hague: Mouton Publishers, 1979).

Taruskin, Richard, 'The Pastness of the Present and the Presence of the Past', in Taruskin, *Text and Act: Essays on Music and Performance* (New York: Oxford University Press, 1995), 90–154.

——, 'Russian Folk Melodies in *The Rite of Spring*', *Journal of the American Musicological Society*, 33/3 (1980), 501–43.

Tick, Judith, 'Charles Ives and Gender Ideology', in Solie (ed.), *Musicology and Difference.*

——, *Ruth Crawford Seeger: A Composer's Search for American Music* (New York: Oxford University Press, 1997), 83–106.

Tomlinson, Gary, 'Gary Tomlinson Responds', *Current Musicology*, 53 (1993), 36–40.

——, *Music in Renaissance Magic: Toward a Historiography of Others* (Chicago: University of Chicago Press, 1993).

——, 'Musical Pasts and Postmodern Musicologies: A Response to Lawrence Kramer', *Current Musicology*, 53 (1992), 18–24.

——, 'The Web of Culture: A Context for Musicology', *19th-Century Music*, 7/3 (1984), 350–62.

Tovey, Donald, 'Beethoven, Symphony in C minor, No. 5, Op. 67', in *Essays in Musical Analysis: Symphonies and other Orchestral Works* (Oxford: Oxford University Press, 1981).

Toynbee, Jason, *Making Popular Music: Musicians, Creativity and Institutions* (London: Arnold, 2000).

Treitler, Leo, 'The Power of Positivist Thinking', *Journal of the American Musicological Society*, 42/2 (1989), 375–402.

Van den Toorn, Pieter, *Music, Politics, and the Academy* (Berkeley: University of California Press, 1995).

Veeser, H. Arram (ed.), *The New Historicism Reader* (New York and London: Routledge, 1994).

Wagner, Richard, 'On Conducting', in *Three Wagner Essays*, trans. Robert L. Jacobs (London: Ernst Eulenburg Ltd, 1979), 49–93.

Walser, Robert, *Running with the Devil: Power, Gender and Madness in Heavy Metal Music* (Hanover, NH: Wesleyan University Press, 1993).

Warhol, Robyn, and Diane Price Herndl (eds), *Feminisms: An Anthology of Literary Theory and Criticism* (New Brunswick, NJ: Rutgers University Press, 1991).

White, Hayden, 'Commentary: Form, Reference, and Ideology in Musical Discourse', in Steven Scher (ed.), *Music and Text: Critical Inquiries* (Cambridge: Cambridge University Press, 1992), 288–319.

Whiteread, Rachel, *House*, ed. James Lingwood (London: Phaidon, 1995).

Williams, Alastair, 'Adorno and the Semantics of Modernism', *Perspectives of New Music*, 37/1 (2001).

——, 'Musicology and Postmodernism', *Music Analysis*, 19/3 (2000), 385–407.

——, *New Music and the Claims of Modernity* (Aldershot: Ashgate, 1997).

Williams, Raymond, 'The Future of Cultural Studies', in Tony Pinkney (ed.), *The Politics of Modernism: Against the New Conformists* (London: Verso, 1989), 151–62.

Žižek, Slavoj, *Looking Awry: An Introduction to Jacques Lacan through Popular Culture* (Cambridge, Mass.: MIT Press, 1992).

——, 'There is no Sexual Relationship', in Renata Saleci and Slavoj Žižek (eds), *Gaze and Voice as Love Objects* (Durham, NC and London: Duke University Press, 1996).

Index